101 WAY:
to
PREPARE KABABS

Satarupa Banerjee

PUSTAK MAHAL®
DELHI • PATNA • BANGALORE
• MUMBAI • HYDERABAD

Publishers

Pustak Mahal®, Delhi

J-3/16 , Daryaganj, New Delhi-110002
☎ 23276539, 23272783, 23272784 • *Fax:* 011-23260518
E-mail: info@pustakmahal.com • *Website:* www.pustakmahal.com

Sales Centre
10-B, Netaji Subhash Marg, Daryaganj, New Delhi-110002
☎ 23268292, 23268293, 23279900 • *Fax:* 011-23280567
E-mail: rapidexdelhi@indiatimes.com

Branch Offices
Bangalore: ☎ 22234025
E-mail: pmblr@sancharnet.in • pustak@sancharnet.in
Mumbai: ☎ 22010941
E-mail: rapidex@bom5.vsnl.net.in
Patna: ☎ 3294193 • *Telefax:* 0612-2302719
E-mail: rapidexptn@rediffmail.com
Hyderabad: *Telefax:* 040-24737290
E-mail: pustakmahalhyd@yahoo.co.in

© **Pustak Mahal, Delhi**

ISBN 81-223-0697-7

Edition : 2006

Printed at : Virgo Press, Delhi

DEDICATION

To my Friend
Gouri Bose, Chef par
excellence
with love and thanks—
it was her Kabab class
that started this collection.

CONTENTS

INTRODUCTION

Nothing is more inviting than the aroma of food cooking on an open fire. And kababs are just that and more.

Kababs have always taken the pride place in Indian cuisine. They have variety and class. You can have them by roadside for a paltry sum or you can shell out an astronomical amount for a more refined version at a 5-Star hotel. Either way, they taste divine.

The Kabab's origin can be traced to the conquests of the mongolian king Chengiz Khan. Chengiz Khan carried the kabab with him from Mongolia to south of Spain and from there to India. The sublimation of the kabab, however, took place with his grandson, Taimur long.

The name Kabab is a combination of two Persian words "kum" (little) and ` aab' (water). Hence obviously kababs are made with very little or no water. Spices and condiments are applied to the meat which is marinated in them for some time and then cooked.

But cooking meat on an open fire finds mention in our ancient treatise, too. 'Susruta Samhita' the ayurvedic treatise describes how food should be tenderised and marinated. Several cooking methods have been described in it including the dressing and roasting of meat over charcoal.

Kababs are cooked in the tandoor, tawa, Kadhai, handi, patila or oven hot coals. And now, in the oven, grill or microwave.

The present day kababs are made from meat, chicken, fish, paneer, vegetables, fruits anything and we have kababs in their infinite avatars. So cook and eat them for lunch, dinner or even at breakfast any time of the day. They make a good meal anytime.

Happy kabab making!

ABBREVIATIONS

gm	-	gram
kg	-	kilogram
l	-	litre
ml	-	millilitre
tsp	-	teaspoon
tbsp	-	tablespoon

WEIGHTS AND MEASURES

Recipes in this book use the standard measuring set of cups and spoons.

A graduated set of four cups measuring one cup, a half, a third and a quarter cup.

A graduated set of 4 spoons—tablespoon, teaspoon, a half and a quarter spoon.

1 tbsp = 3 tsp   1 cup = 16 tbsp

All measurements are level unless stated otherwise.

Here are a few tips on how to measure.

Liquids: Place the measuring cup on a flat surface and pour the liquid to the required level. The spoons should also be filled to the level.

Dry Ingredients: These should be spooned lightly into the cup until heaped, then levelled off with a straight edged knife or spatula. Never pack the ingredients down or shake or tap the cup. And unless specified, measure before shifting.

Moist Ingredients: These ingredients, like shortening and brown sugar, have to be packed in lightly. Press the fat into the cup so that air spaces are forced out. Level fat to straighten edge when full.

How To Go About Preparing The Perfect Kabab

Three points are most important in the preparation of kababs. 1. The quality and blending of spices in the marinade. 2. The quality of meat, the cut selected. 3. The precise timing in the actual cooking.

Overcooking the kabab must be avoided. Whenever one starts cooking the meat, the temparature should be higher for the meat to sear on the surface. This helps to retain the juices. Then cook at a lower temparature till the meat is cooked through.

There are various ways of cooking the kabab. The tandoor, mahi tawa (copper vessel for shallow frying), Kadhai, handi, dum, tawa and sigrhi (coal oven). The tandoor (north Indian clay oven) is probably the most versatile kitchen equipment in the world.

Today, one can get gas tandoor, which, as the name implies, can be put on the gas and works most efficiently. And of course, there's the grill, oven and microwave; all these can be used most effectively to cook the kabab.

A tawa made of thick gauge iron is better than aluminium or stainless steel which lets food burn more quickly. A non-stick tawa is a good buy as heat is distributed more evenly to allow uniform cooking without burning.

The importance of marinades in kabab making cannot be over emphasised. Marinades help keep the meat tender and succulent. The duration of the marination depends on the size and texture of the meat. For instance, a tikka of fish will be ready to roast in 30 minutes, while a whole fish takes around 2–3 hours. Similarly a boti of lamb may be marinated for 2–3 hours, while a whole leg of lamb takes at least 12 hours, which means that the fibrous meat requires a longer marination than either chicken or fish.

Marinades can be sweet, savoury, spicy or fruity. Use oil marinades for dry foods such as lean meat or white fish,

11

vinegar based marinades for rich food with higher fat contents. Add salt just before cooking. The curd used in the marinade should be hung to drain the whey. Otherwise, the marinade becomes too watery resulting in bland kababs.

Use marinades for basting or brushing the food while cooking. It is important to bring food to room temparature before grilling. Do not overcook. Serve immediately. Dry heat grilling is best for fish with lots of oil, such as salmon and tuna. Lean fish requires basting to keep it moist.

Choose fish with firm flesh or it might break up and drop as you turn it. Wrap delicate fish like hilsa in aluminium foil or banana leaves to cook in its own juice. Seafood cooks fast and does not need to be left long in a marinade.

Large joints of meat or poultry can be parboiled and finished on coals or grilled. The juice should run clear when the meat is cooked.

Oil the cooking vessel, be it the grill racks or the tawa, before cooking, so that the food doesn't stick to it. Always taste the food to make sure it is cooked thoroughly before serving.

Personally, I don't like to use food colour in cooking. The bright red or orange coloured tandoori food you eat, owes its hue to food colours. You may use it, if you desire, but see to it that you buy approved food grade colours.

For best results, use long handled utensils-fork, spatula, basting brush and tongs.

Keep a table nearby to hold serving platters, an oven mitt, and marinades and sauces.

Always heat the tandoor or oven for 5 minutes before cooking.

Try not to pierce meat often as juices will be lost.

Soak wooden skewers in water for 30 minutes prior to piercing with meat or vegetables.

VEGETARIAN KABABS

ALOO LAJAWAAB
(STUFFED POTATOES)

Serve with a sweet sour anardana chutney; it will add to an already fine preparation.

Ingredients (Serves 4)

- 8 large potatoes
- 1/2 cup thick curd
- 1/2 tsp turmeric
- 1 tbsp chaat masala, pinch of saffron, black salt to taste
- 1 tbsp coriander seeds
- 1 tbsp cuminseeds
- 2 dry red chillies

For Filling
- 4 tbsp grated coconut
- 8 tbsp grated paneer
- 4 tbsp coarsely chopped walnuts
- 4 tbsp chopped raisins
- 2 green chillies, finely chopped
- 2 tsp sugar, salt to taste
- 1 tbsp refined oil
- 1 tsp grated ginger
- 2 cups of water

Preparation

Parboil the potatoes. peel and cut a slice from the tops. Reserve the tops. Scoop out the middle portions carefully.

Filling: Heat the oil in a small karahi and temper with the ginger and green chillis. Add the other ingredients and scooped out potatoes and stir fry, till well mixed.

Fill the potatoes with this mixture and fix the caps with toothpicks. Lightly roast and crush the cumin, coriander and red chillies. Beat the curd and add the turmeric, powdered spices, chaat masala and salt; pour the mixture over the potatoes coating thickly.

Drizzle a little oil over the potatoes an©d cook in a hot tandoor for 20-25 minutes or till the potatoes are somewhat dry, coated with the spices and well done; alternatively, bake in a hot oven - 200°C/400°F for 15-20 minutes.

Gajrela Kabab (Carrot Kabab)

Most of us imagine kababs to be barbecued outdoors, but it can turn into a lip smacking treat indoors with this wonderful carrot kabab.

Ingredients (Serves 4)
- 250 gm carrots
- 50 gm onion, a handful of chopped coriander leaves
- 2 green chillies
- 1/3 cup grated khoya
- 2 tbsp chopped cashewnuts
- 2 tbsp chopped raisins
- 1 tbsp powdered anardana
- salt to taste, dry breadcrumbs as needed, refined oil for frying
- 1 cup gram flour

Preparation
Scrape and grate the carrots and finely chop the onions and green chillies.

Mix all the ingredients together except the breadcrumbs and oil.

Moisten your hands and form sausage shaped kababs from the mixture. Roll in dry breadcrumbs and deep fry in hot oil till golden brown.

Serve hot with a sweet sour chutney and a raita.

These kababs can also be coated with semolina or crushed vemicelli and fried.

GRILLED VEGETABLES

It seems, no book of kabab, these days, can be complete without grilled vegetables. Serve them as a side dish with fish, meat or chicken kababs or as an appetiser.

Ingredients

- Asparagus spears
- baby carrots, baby corn
- brinjal
- capsicum
- small potatoes
- pumpkin
- cauliflower florets
- tomato
- spring onion

Preparation

Rinse, trim, cut up and precook vegetables. To precook any vegetable - bring a small amount of water to boil. Add desired vegetable and simmer, covered till crisp tender. Drain well.

To grill, brush the vegetables with oil or butter. Grease grill rack as well. Cook vegetables till tender and slightly charred, turning occasionally.

Serve sprinkled with lime juice and chaat masala, if desired.

Vegetables like asparagus, cauliflower, carrots, and potato need parboiling. Do not precook capsicum, baby corn, spring onion or brinjal.

Paneer Shashlik

Given the rise in vegetarianism and health consciousness this delicious paneer shashlik is just the thing.

Ingredients (Serves 6)

- 200 gm paneer, cut into 2.5 cm (1") cubes
- 1 cup pineapple cubes
- 1 cup capsicum cubes
- 1 cup onion wedges
- 1 cup tomato cubes
- Butter as needed

For Sauce
- ¾ cup cream
- 1 tbsp ginger green chilli paste
- 1 tbsp flour
- 1½ tsp kewra water
- 1 tbsp lime juice
- ¼ tsp sugar
- ¼ tsp salt
- ½ tsp chilli powder
- ¼ tsp ajwain
- ¼ tsp black salt
- ½ tsp cumin powder

Kabab Masala
- 1 tsp chaat masala
- ½ tsp kasuri methi
- ¼ tsp garam masala pd. Mix and use

Preparation

Mix all the ingredients for the sauce together. Marinate the paneer pieces in it for half an hour. Put through the skewers alongwith the pineapple and vegetables. Brush with melted butter and then with the marinade.

Roast the shashliks over hot coals, brushing with the sauce and turning frequently. Alternatively, fry with a little butter on a tawa.

Sprinkle on top the kabab masala and serve hot.

.IVER KABAB
↓

↑ BEMISAL KABAB

ALOO LAJAWAB
↓

↑ HUSSAINY KABAB

← BEIDA KABAB

↓ MAHI KABAB

HARIYALI KABAB
(GREEN PEA KABAB)

As you bite into the kabab, you get a whiff of the coriander and garam masala. The chillis and cheese in the kabab tantalise the taste buds.

Ingredients (Serves 4-6)

- 1 cup pulpy paneer
- 1 cup green pea paste
- 2 tbsp refined oil
- 3 slices of bread
- 4 green chillies, finely chopped
- a large handful of finely chopped fresh coriander
- salt to taste
- 1 ½ tsp amchur
- ½ tsp garam masala powder
- ¼ cup grated cheese, refined oil for frying

Preparation

Blend the paneer and green peas together.

Heat the oil in a non-stick karahi and add the paneer mixture. Fry over medium low heat till it forms a ball.

Dip the bread slices in water and squeeze to get rid of excess moisture. Add the bread, green chillies, fresh coriander, salt, amchur and garam masala powder to the paneer and pea mix. Blend well.

Divide into small balls. Fill each with a little grated cheese. Deep fry till golden brown.

Serve with chutney or sauce.

Variation: You may stuff the kabab with finely chopped coriander and green chillies slaked in lime juice instead of the cheese.

NUTRI KABAB

For the vegetarians who miss out on the shami kabab.

Ingredients (Makes 12)

- 100 gm soyabean chunks
- 150 gm Bengal gram dal
- 1 tbsp ginger paste
- 1 tsp garlic paste
- 4 slices of bread
- ½ tsp black cardamom powder
- ½ tsp garam masala powder
- 1 tsp amchur or chaat masala
- 1 tsp salt
- 1 large onion, finely chopped
- ½ cup chopped fresh coriander
- 4 green chillies, finely chopped, refined oil for frying

Preparation

Soak the soyabean chunks in hot water for 1 hour. Drain and squeeze out water. Pressure cook with 3 cups of water for 10 minutes. Squeeze the nuaggets once more to get rid of all moisture.

Cook dal with ginger - garlic paste and just enough water to cover. Do not overcook; dry excess moisture, if any.

Grind the soya nuggets and dal separately. Then grind together again with the bread, chilli powder, cardamom powder, garam masala powder, amchur and salt. Mix onion and fresh coriander.

Prepare 12 kababs. Deep fry in hot oil or shallow fry in a non-stick tawa.

NUT KABAB

Here is a kabab that deserves all the culinary superlatives.

Ingredients (Serves 4)
* 1 cup milk
* 1 ½ tbsp butter
* 2 ½ tbsp flour
* salt to taste
* 1 tsp cumin powder
* ½ tsp chilli powder
* 2 green chillies finely chopped
* 2 tbsp chopped fresh coriander
* 4 slices bread, made into crumbs
* 1 cup crushed nuts a mix of almonds, cashewnuts, peanuts, walnuts and magaj
* 1 onion, sliced and fried
* dry breadcrumbs as needed, refined oil for frying
* Batter–¼ cup flour
* salt and pepper

Preparation
Boil the milk with butter. Add flour. Cook till it leaves the sides of the vessel, stirring continuously. Cool.

Add salt, cumin, chillies, green chillies, coriander leaves, fresh bread crumbs, nuts, and fried onion. Mix properly. Form into tikias or sausage shapes.

Prepare a thin batter with the seasoned flour and water. Dip the prepared kabab in it, letting extra batter drip. Deep fry in hot oil till golden.

PANEER TIKKA

Ingredients (Serves 4)
- 300 gm Paneer

Marinade
- 120 ml cream
- 2 cubes of cheese, grated
- 1 tbsp ginger–garlic paste
- 1 ½ tbsp cornflour, generous pinch of mace and green cardamom powder each
- ½ tsp chilli powder
- ½ tsp cumin powder
- ½ tsp powdered ajwain
- ½ tsp pepper

For Topping
- 1 tbsp kasoori methi
- ½ tsp black salt
- 1 tsp roasted and powdered cumin
- 1 tsp amchur

Preparation
Lightly roast the kasoori methi and crush. Mix all the topping ingredients and reserve.

Cut the paneer in 3 cm square pieces. Prick each cube lightly with a fork.

Mix all the ingredients for the marinade and marinate the paneer pieces in it for 3–4 hours.

Thread the paneer pieces using fine skewers, (you can also use previously soaked, cleaned broomsticks) 5–6 cubes each. Keep a distance between each cube.

Grill, rotating and basting till done—the paneer pieces should look dry and a bit charred. Can be cooked on open fire or tandoor, too.

Remove from skewers. Sprinkle with the topping spices and serve at once.

VEGETABLE GULAR KABAB

Ingredients (Makes 12–15)
- 120 gm Bengal gram dal
- 6 large raw bananas, pinch of saffron mixed with 1 tbsp milk
- 4 green chillies
- ½ cup coriander leaves
- 3 tbsp hung curd, salt and pepper to taste
- ½ tsp cumin powder
- 1 tsp chilli powder, pinch of mace and green cardamom powder each
- 1 tbsp roasted gram flour
- 1 tsp chaat masala, poppy seeds as needed, refined oil for frying

For Stuffing
- 2 tbsp raisins
- 2 green chillis
- 1 tsp fresh corinader, finely chop and soak in 1 tbsp lime juice

Preparation

Cook the gram dal and bananas separately till just done. On no account they should be overcooked. Drain the dal. Peel and grate the banana. Heat the saffron and mix with the milk. Finely chop the green chillies and fresh coriander.

Blend the dal, banana, green chillies, fresh coriander salt and pepper in the mixie till well blended; mix the rest of the ingredients and knead well.

Shape into balls and stuff a little of the filling. Roll again to a smooth ball.

Place the poppy seeds on a tray and roll the kababs so that they are well coated.

Heat enough oil in a karahi and fry till golden.

Make a bed of shredded lettuce or cabbage leaves and serve the kababs on them with a sweet sour anardana chutney.

VEGETABLE TANDOORI

Sheekh kabab of exotic vegetables.

Ingredients

- 200 gm button mushrooms
- 3 capsicums, 1green, 1 red and 1 yellow, preferably
- 8 baby corns
- 8 broccoli florets

Marinade
- 2 tsp gram flour
- 1 tsp tandoori chaat masala
- 1 tsp yellow chilli powder
- ½ tsp red chilli powder
- 1 tsp ginger garlic paste, juice of 1 lime
- 1 tbsp refined oil
- 1 tsp malt vinegar
- salt to taste
- 1 pinch of powdered caraway seeds

Preparation

Cut the stalks, clean and blanch the mushrooms. Deseed and cut the capsicum in square pieces, slightly larger than the mushrooms.

Halve each baby corn; cut the broccoli in medium sized florets.

Mix all the ingredients for the marinade adding a few drops of water. Marinate the vegetables, coating well, for 3 hours.

Pierce the vegetables on a thin skewer alernating mushrooms and vegetables decoratively.

Cook in tandoor or grill in oven, basting with the marinade and a few drops of oil. Turn the skewers a few times in between to ensure that all the sides are cooked.

Remove from skewers and serve hot.

Variation: You may vary the marinade, choosing any other from this book.

Phaldhari Seekh Kabab
(Vegetarian Seekh Kabab)

Ingredients (Makes 12 Kababs)

- 200 gm yam
- 2 medium potatoes
- 1 large carrot
- 100 gm paneer
- 15 french beans
- 12 alubukharas (dry plums)
- 12 anjeer (dried figs)
- 2 tbsp chopped coriander leaves
- 2 tsp grated ginger
- 1 tbsp Kashmiri chilli powder
- 1 tsp anardana powder
- 1 tsp black salt
- ½ tsp sugar
- 1 tsp roasted and powdered cumin
- 2 green chillies finely chopped, refined oil for frying

Preparation

Boil the yam and potatoes, but take care not to overcook. Peel and grate while still hot. Scrap and grate carrot. Grate paneer. String, blanch and finely chop the beans.

Soak the alubukharas and figs for 1 hour. Deseed the alubukharas and finely chop alongwith the figs.

Knead all the ingredients except oil thoroughly to a dough. Divide into 12 balls using a moist hand. Shape each ball into 10 cm long kababs (like sheekh kabab).

Heat enough oil in a karahi and deep fry the kababs, till golden. Serve with a chutney or dip.

SHAKAHARI KABAB
(PANEER KABAB)

The Combination of pomegranate and dill gives this kabab an extraordinary refreshisng flavour.

Ingredients (Serves 4)

- 500 gm paneer, cubed
- 12 button mushrooms
- 3 large capsicums
- 2–3 slices pineapple
- 1 large onion
- 2 large tomatoes, butter or ghee for frying

Marinade

- ¼ cup pomegranate juice
- 2 tsp lime juice
- 2 tbsp refined oil
- 2 tbsp chopped dill
- 1 tsp dry pomegranate seed pd
- 1 tsp amchur
- 1 tsp chilli powder
- ½ tsp powdered caraway seeds
- Salt to taste

Preparation

Remove the stems of the mushrooms and blanch in boiling salted water for 2 minutes. Drain.

Deseed and cut the capsicum in 2.5 cm square pieces. Using red, green and yellow capsicum gives a better visual effect.

Drain the syrup from pineapple slices and dice. Peel the onion and cut into 3 pieces. Separate and remove 16 large petals. Deseed and quarter the tomatoes and cut each quarter in 2 pieces.

Marination: Mix all the ingredients and rub the kabab ingredients with it and keep aside for 30 minutes.

Take clean broomsticks, skewer all the ingredients 3 each, decoratively.

Take a non-stick tawa, heat 1 tbsp butter or ghee and fry the kababs for 6–8 minutes rotating. The paneer and pineapple should pick up brown spots.

Serve immediately with any fruity dip.

Raw Banana Kabab

Aromatic and spicy.

Ingredients (Serves 4)

- 8 raw bananas
- 2 medium potatoes
- 1.5 cm piece of ginger
- 100 gm onion
- 5 green chillies
- 2 tbsp coriander leaves
- 50 gm Bengal gram dal
- 1 tsp garam masala powder
- salt to taste
- 1 tsp amchur, juice of 1 lime
- 100 gm fresh breadcrumbs, refined oil for frying

Preparation

Boil the bananas and potatoes. But do not over cook and no pressure cooking either. Peel and grate them. Grate the ginger and very finely chop the green chillies and coriander leaves.

Boil the gram dal and grind to a paste. Mix all the ingredients together except the oil and knead to make a soft dough. Shape into tikias.

Heat the oil in a non-stick frying pan and shallow fry the tikki as over medium heat until golden brown and crisp. On both the sides. Remove onto absorbent paper.

Serve hot with chutney.

Shaped into tiny kababs, they make very good cocktail snacks. Dot each kabab with a little ketchup or chutney and pierce with a cocktail stick.

Motia Tikki
(Pearl Balls)

The Sago looks like pearls, hence the name.

Ingredients (Serves 6)

- 150 gm small sized sago
- 100 gm carrots, French beans and cauli flower each
- 2 medium potatoes
- 2 raw bananas
- salt to taste
- 1 tsp chilli powder
- 1 tsp garam masala powder
- 1 tsp cumin powder
- 1 heaped tsp amchur, a handful of chopped fresh coriander, chaat masala as needed, refined oil for frying

Preparation

Wash and soak the sago for 10 minutes. Spread on a tray to dry. Grate the carrot and cauliflower. Very finely chop the beans. Boil potatoes and raw bananas till almost done. Do not overcook. Peel and grate.

Heat 1 tsp oil in a pan. Season with the cuminseeds. Add the carrot, bean and cauliflower. Stir fry for 2 minutes; put in the salt, chilli, garam masala and cumin powder. Stir till dry.

When cool enough to handle, mix the potato, banana, amchur and coriander. Knead to a soft dough. Divide into small tikkis. Roll over the sago to coat well.

Heat enough oil in a karahi. Put in a few tikkis at a time and fry till golden. Remove onto an absorbent paper to drain excess oil.

Sprinkle with chaat masala and serve hot with a raita and/or salad.

These tikkis can be used in pulaos; it makes good cocktail snacks as well.

PANEER KE CHUTNEYWALE SULE (PANEER KABAB WITH GREEN CHUTNEY)

You may add baby potatoes, baby corns, pearl onions and cherry tomatoes.

Ingredients (Serves 4)
- 10 button mushrooms
- 10 water chestnuts
- 10 cubes of brinjals
- 200 gm cubed paneer
- 1 tsp salt
- oil for basting

For Chutney
- 50 gm mint, leaves only
- 100 gm fresh coriander, leaves only
- 2 tsp cuminseed
- 4 green chillies
- 2 large tomatoes, black salt to taste

Preparation
Scrub, wash and dry the mushrooms. Peel and keep the water chestnuts whole. Sprinkle salt all over the vegetables and paneer pieces.

Grind the ingredients for the chutney together. Marinate the paneer and vegetables in it for 20 minutes.

Skewer and cook over charcoal fire or grill brushing with the chutney and basting with oil for 10 minutes.

MASOOR KABAB
(LENTIL KABAB)

There is more to kababs than meat or chicken. Try this vegetarian version and decide for yourself.

Ingredients (Serves 6)
- 1 cup whole lentils with husk (kala masoor ki dal chilkewale)
- 2.5 cm piece of ginger
- 6 cloves of garlic
- 6 green chillies
- ½ tsp cuminseeds, refined oil
- 1 tsp amchur
- ½ tsp garam masala powder
- salt to taste
- ⅓ cup fresh coriander leaves
- 1 tsp kewra water
- 3 slices of bread

Preparation
Soak the lentils overnight. Drain and grind alongwith ginger, garlic and green chillies without any additional water. The paste should be very fine.

Heat 2 tbsp oil in a karahi and add the dal paste. Stir-fry till it forms a ball and leaves the sides of the vessel. Cool.

Then add the amchur, garam masala powder, salt, fresh coriander and kewra water. Dip the bread slices in water and squeeze to get rid of excess moisture. Mix well with the dal, mixing well with your hands.

Form into sausage shaped kababs. Deep fry in oil till golden.

Serve with roasted papad, fresh salad and green chutney.

HARABHARA KABAB
(SPINACH KABAB)

Kababs used to mean non-vegetarian fare. Now-a-days, with the accent on vegetarianism, kababs made of vegetables are gaining popularity. The following is an excellent one.

Ingredients (Serves 4)

- 3 bunches spinach
- 100 gm Bengal gram dal
- 4 green chillies, chopped
- 2 tsp grated ginger, juice of 1 lime
- 1 tsp anardana powder, salt to taste, refined oil for frying

For Filling
- 1/3 cup paneer
- 2 tbsp finely chopped cashewnuts
- 1 tbsp fnely chopped raisins
- 1 tbsp coriander leaves
- 1 tsp chaat masala
- salt to taste

Preparation

Mash the paneer and mix with all the remaining ingredients.

Clean the spinach of all discoloured or wilted leaves. Discard the stems. Blanch in enough boiling water. Squeeze to get rid of all moisture. Grind to a paste without adding water.

Soak the gram dal for 4 hours and cook till done. Strain and grind to a paste.

Mix all the ingredients. Heat 2 tsp oil in a non-stick skillet and saute the spinach paste. Stir till dry and it forms a ball.

Divide the spinach paste into large lime sized balls. Divide the filling in equal number of balls. Pat one part of the spinach into a circle, shape into a cup and put one part of the filling in it. Roll to cover the filling completely. Flatten to shape like tikkis. Likewise prepare all the kababs.

Heat enough oil on a tawa, preferably non-stick. Shallow fry the kababs.

Pahari Kabab
(Yam Kabab)

Once you've tasted this vegetarian version of shami kabab do not be surprised, if you never mince matters again.

Ingredients (Serves 6–8)
- 5 tbsp Bengal gram dal
- 1 kg yam
- 2.5 cm ginger
- 15 cloves garlic
- 6 green chillies
- 1 tbsp coriander seeds
- 2 tsp fennel seeds
- 2 pieces of cinnamon
- 5 cloves
- 3 black cardamoms
- 2 onions
- 2 tsp salt, juice of 1 lime, refined oil for frying, a handful of fresh coriander

Preparation
Soak the dal in water for 3 hours. Peel and cut yam into cubes. Pressure cook the yam and dal for 8–10 minutes. Drain water completely.

Very lightly roast all the spices and grind to a powder. Finely chop the onions and green chillies.

Grind the yam and dal. Mix with all the ingredients very well using your hands. Prepare small tikkias out of it and shallow fry on a tawa till golden brown.

Serve with a chutney, preferably anardana chutney.

KHILE PHOOL
(CAULIFLOWER KABAB)

Ingredients (Serves 6)

- 1 large cauliflower, cut into florets
- ½ coconut, grated
- 1 tbsp cuminseeds
- 6 red chillies
- 2 black cardamoms
- 5 cm piece of ginger
- 2 cloves of garlic
- 3 tbsp malt vinegar
- 1 tbsp refined oil or ghee
- 1 tsp salt

Preparation

Grind together the coconut, cuminseeds, red chillies, black cardamoms (seed only), ginger and garlic to a smooth paste. Mix the vinegar, oil and salt.

Parboil the cauliflorets for 5 minutes in salted water. Drain and marinate in the ground mixture for 15 minutes.

Skewer and grill basting with oil or ghee till crisp tender. Serve hot sprinkled with lime juice.

CHICKEN KABABS

MAKHMALI MURG KABAB (STUFFED CHICKEN KABAB)

Ingredients (Serves 6–8)

- 8 boneless chicken breasts, salt to taste
- ½ tsp chilli powder
- 2 tsp ginger garlic paste

For Filling

- 1 small onion
- 200 gm chicken mince
- 1 tbsp refined oil
- ½ tsp garam masala powder
- salt to taste
- 10 cashewnuts, chopped
- 10 raisins, chopped
- a handful of chopped coriander leaves
- 1 tsp cumin powder
- ½ tsp chilli powder
- 2 cubes cheese, grated

For Batter

- 150 gm flour
- 2 eggs
- salt and pepper to taste

Preparation

Flatten the chicken breasts in between two plastic sheets with the help of a meat mallet. Rub in the salt, chilli powder and ginger garlic paste.

Filling: Heat the oil in a kadahi and saute the onion for 5 minutes. Add the mince garam masala powder, salt, cashewnuts raisins, coriander leaves, cumin and chilli powder. Stir fry for 3–4 minutes. Sprinkle ¼ cup of hot water. Cover and cook till done. The mixture should be dry. When cool, add the grated cheese.

Take a flattened breast. Place $1/_8$ of the filling in the middle and fold the breast envelope fashion till well covered. Close the opening with a toothpick.

Prepare all the breasts this way. Wrap each with aluminium foil securely. Cook in a tandoor or a moderately hot oven for 15 minutes.

Batter: Beat the egg yolks, then beat in the flour, salt and pepper. Whip the egg whites till stiff and fold into the batter.

Dip the cooked chicken breasts (after removing the picks) in this batter and deep fry till golden. Cut each in two and serve hot with a salad and a sauce.

TANDOORI FISH

SPICY KABAB →

TANDOORI CHIKEN
WITH DIFFERENCE

NAWABI KABAB

CHUTNEY CHOP ↓

CHATPATA MURG KABAB
(SPICY CHICKEN KABAB)

Continuous basting kababs with the marinade is most important as it prevents them from drying out and become leathery.

Ingredients (Serves 4)
- ½ kg boneless chicken, cut in strips
- 1 large can pineapple
- ¼ cup light soya sauce
- 1 tbsp tomato ketchup
- 1 tsp chilli sauce
- 2 tbsp honey or brown sugar
- 1 tsp grated ginger
- 1 clove of garlic, crushed salt to taste
- 1 capsicum, cut into cubes

Preparation
Cut the pineapple slices into small cubes. Combine the soya sauce, ketchup, chilli sauce, honey or brown sugar, ginger and garlic. Taste and add salt, if needed, because all the sauces are salted.

Add the chicken and mix well. Refrigerate overnight, if possible or at least for 2–3 hours.

Drain chicken, Thread chicken, pineapple and capsicum onto skewers. Barbecue or grill in an oven, brushing with the marinade till done.

Serve on a bed of lettuce.

Combine the same amount of the marinade freshly. Heat for 2 minutes and pass with the kabab as the dipping sauce.

TANDOORI CHICKEN WITH A DIFFERENCE

This recipe draws its inspiration from Russian cuisine, Georgia particularly. Georgian cuisine is at once earthy and sophisticated, exotic and exquisite. The delightful sweet tart plum sauce, so much part of Georgian cooking, is a perfect foil for the chicken.

Ingredients (Serves 4)

- 1 large chicken, aprox. 1.5 kg, cut into 8 pieces
- 1 cup hung curd
- 1 tsp cumin powder
- 1 tsp coriander powder
- 1 tsp chilli powder
- 1 tbsp ginger paste
- 1 tbsp kasuri methi powder
- salt to taste
- ghee or butter as needed
- 2 tbsp chopped herbs (coriander, dill and basil)
- Sweet sour plum sauce: 250 gm sour plums
- 2 tbsp finely chopped fresh coriander, a handful of basil, chopped
- 2 sprigs dill, finely chopped
- ¼ tsp salt
- 1 cup sugar
- 1 tsp chilli powder

Preparation

Dry the chicken pieces absolutely. Slit at a few places. Beat the curd in a bowl. Add the rest of the ingredients except ghee or butter. Add the chicken and refrigerate for as long as time permits, at least 5–6 hours.

Take out chicken from the marinade and cook in a tandoor brushing with ghee or butter and basting with the marinade till done. Serve with plum sauce.

Sweet sour plum Sauce: Wash add plums and cook in very little water and a pinch of salt till very soft. Remove the pits and blend to a puree.

Finely chop the herbs and add to the puree alongwith the remaining ingredients. Boil till thick. Remove and cool.

Murg Ke Achari Parche

A zingy starter to set the mood for your next cocktail party.

Ingredients (Serves 4)
- ³/₄ tsp kalonji
- ³/₄ tsp aniseed
- 75 ml mustard oil
- ³/₄ tsp fenugreek, seeds
- 1 tsp yellow chilli powder
- 1 tbsp ginger paste
- 4 tsp gram flour
- 1 tbsp garlic paste
- ¼ tsp garam masala powder
- salt to taste
- 500 g boneless pieces of chicken
- 2 tbsp pickle

Preparation
Soak the kalonji, aniseed and fenugreek seeds in mustard oil for 2 days prior to cooking. Mix pickle with 1 tbsp water for 15 minutes mash and strain to get the juice.

Combine the gram flour, mustard oil mix, chilli powder, ginger garlic paste, garam masala powder, pickle juice and salt. Mix this thoroughly with the chicken pieces. Keep aside for 4 hours.

Skewer and cook over charcoal fire or in a hot oven or tandoor. You may also saute them in a non-stick frying pan.

Serve with onion rings and a green salad.

Murg Anari Kabab
(Pomegranate Flavoured
Chicken Kabab)

Using fresh fruit juices in the marinades not only helps to tenderise the meat, but it is also a delicious way of imparting a fruity flavour to the kabab.

Ingredients (Serves 6)
- 2 chicken legs
- 2 chicken thighs
- 2 chicken breasts
- ½ cup fresh pomegranate juice
- 1 tbsp chilli sauce
- 1 tsp grated lime rind
- 1 tbsp lime juice
- 1 tbsp vinegar
- 1 tbsp molasses or brown sugar or honey
- salt and pepper to taste
- 1 tsp cornflour

Preparation
Make a few slits on the chicken pieces. Combine the rest of the ingredients except cornflour. Marinate the chicken in it for at least 4 hours, preferably longer.

Drain the chicken one hour before cooking. Put in a little oil and grill or cook in a tandoor, basting with the marinade, till tender.

Combine a fresh amount of the marinating ingredients. Blend the cornflour with it and heat until the sauce boils and thickens.

Serve with the anari kababs.

BARBECUED CHICKEN LEGS

Winter evenings are ideal for a barbecue in the garden or out on the terrace.

Ingredients (Serves 4)

- 8 chicken drumsticks, juice of 1 lime
- 1 tbsp refined oil or butter
- 1 cup thick curd
- 1 tbsp ginger—garlic paste
- ¼ tsp garam masala powder
- salt to taste

For Filling

- ¼ cup cream
- ¼ cup grated cheese
- 2 tbsp green chillis, minced
- 2 tbsp very finely chopped cashewnuts
- ¼ tsp garam masala powder, pinch of salt

Preparation

Wash and dry the drumsticks. With your fingers, probe the drumsticks from the bone end gently. You will find the flesh give away and form a pocket. Sprinkle with lime juice inside out. Stuff the pockets with a little of the filling. Prepare all the drumsticks the same way.

Filling: Mix all the ingredient together.

To Cook: Hang the curd tied in a muslin till almost all the whey drains off. Beat the hung curd and add the ginger garlic paste, garam masala powder. Salt and oil. Marinate the drumsticks in it for an hour.

Wrap each leg individually in foil and barbecue on high heat for 20 minutes, turning often. Remove foil and roast again for 10 minutes till the legs are done and coloured.

If you barbecue on coal instead of grilling you get a lovely smoky flavour.

Narangi Tikka
(Chicken Kababs with Oranges)

Marinating kababs in citrus fruit juices like orange or sweet lime is becoming very popular today as people are getting diet conscious. This gives a fresh flavour and the marinade can later be used in the sauce to serve with as well as to baste it.

Ingredients (Serves 6)

- 12 breasts of chicken, boneless

I. Marinade
- 1 tbsp ginger paste
- 2 tsp garlic paste
- 1 cup fresh orange juice
- 1 tsp lime juice
- ½ tsp salt
- 1 tsp sugar

II. Marinade
- 1 orange
- 4 green chillis, 1 egg
- ½ cup grated cheese
- 1½ tbsp cashewnut paste
- 2 tbsp very finely chopped fresh coriander genorous pinch of powdered mace
- ¼ tsp grated nutmeg
- 1 tsp salt
- 150 ml cream

Preparation

Skin and cut the chicken breasts in thick cubes. Prick a few times with a fork.

I. Marination: Mix ginger garlic paste with ¼ cup of orange juice. Strain and mix with the remaining ingredients. Soak the chicken pieces in this marinade, rubbing well and reserve for 2 hours.

II. Marination: Peel, discard seeds and membrances and divide the orange into segments. Deseed and very finely chop the green chillis.

Beat the egg in a bowl. Add the cheese and mix well. Now, add the rest of the ingredients and stir to mix. The orange segments should get broken and evenly distributed. Finally stir in the cream. Add 1 tsp sugar, if the orange is sour.

38

Take out the chicken cubes from the first marinade. Shake off the excess moisture and rub with the second marinade. Refrigerate for as long as possible 4–8 hours.

Skewer the chicken pieces divided between 6 skewers. Keep a tray underneath to collect the drippings.

Grill in a preheated 250°C/450°F oven, rotating and basting for 6–8 minutes.

Can also be cooked in a tandoor or over live characoals.

Variation: Paneer cubes can be barbecued the same way. In that case, omit the garlic paste and add 1 tsp powdered dry rose petals in the second marinade.

BOTI KABAB

Chicken breasts make the most succulent kababs, though all of the chicken cut into boneless cubes can be used for economy.

Ingredients (Serves 4–6)

- 4 whole chicken breasts, or 1 whole chicken deboned and cut into small cubes

I.   Marinade
- salt to taste, juice of 2 lemons

II.   Marinade
- ½ cup thick curd
- 6 cloves of garlic
- 50 gm ginger
- ½ tsp cumin powder
- 1 tsp chilli powder
- 1 tsp garam masala powder
- ¼ cup cashewnut paste
- ¼ cup cream
- 2 tsp ghee or butter

Preparation

Rub the chicken cubes with salt and lime juice and set aside for 1 hour.

Second marinade: Grind together the ginger and garlic. Whip the curd till smooth and mix with the remaining ingredients. Soak the chicken pieces in it for 8–12 hours, as time permits.

Half an hour before serving, thread the chicken pieces on skewers or previously soaked bamboo sticks. Do not put more than 6 pieces of chicken per skewer. Do not leave a lot of space between the botis.

Bake in the gas tandoor or over charcoal, basting frequently with the marinade or till done about 8–10 minutes.

You may cook a few of the skewers at a time, depending on the size of the tandoor.

The kababs may be grilled in the oven, too.

The kababs can be served on the skewers or taken off and the botis served on a plate lined with lettuce leaves and garnished with onion rings, lemon wedges and sprigs of mint.

BAKED KABAB

A rather innovative dish. The chicken pieces are baked in a spicy sauce resulting in succulent kababs. It's not always possible to skewer and grill kababs. This recipe comes handy then.

Ingredients (Serves 4)

- 1 chicken
- salt to taste, juice of 1 lime
- 2 onions
- 2.5 cm ginger
- 10 cloves of garlic
- 1 cup curd
- 1 tbsp ketchup
- 1 tsp chilli powder
- ½ tsp garam masala powder
- 1 tsp sugar
- 2 tbsp butter or oil

For Sauce
- 2 large tomatoes
- 2 tbsp butter
- 1 tbsp flour
- 1 cup of water
- ¼ cup tomato ketchup
- ½ tsp chilli powder
- ½ tsp garam masala
- 1 tsp sugar
- salt to taste
- 2 cubes cheese, grated

Preparation

Clean and wash chicken and cut in 16 pieces. Pat dry; rub with salt and lime juice.

Mince the onion, ginger and garlic. Mix the curd, onion, ginger, garlic, ketchup, chilli powder, garam masala, sugar and butter or oil.

Marinate the chicken in it for 4 hours or preferably overnight.

Sauce: Blanch the tomatoes, deseed and blend to a puree.

Heat the butter in a karahi. Add the flour and fry till the raw smell disappears; about a minute. Gradually add the stock or water, stirring constantly so that no lumps form.

Remove from the heat and mix in the tomato puree, ketchup, chilli powder, sugar, garam masala and salt. Put on a low heat and cook for 2–3 minutes.

Finale: Grease a baking dish. Place the chicken with the marinade and bake for 20 minutes turning a few times in between. If you find it drying out, baste with a little of the sauce.

Pour in the sauce, turn the chicken pieces to coat well and bake for a further 15 minutes.

Sprinkle the cheese and bake for a further 10 minutes. By this time the chicken should be absolutely tender.

Serve hot.

TALI HUI TIKKA
(FRIED CHICKEN NUGGETS)

A welcome variation of the ubiquitous chicken tikka kabab.

Ingredients (Serves 6)

- 500 gm boneless chicken, cut into medium cubes
- 1 lt. milk, pinch of saffron
- ½ tsp salt
- refined oil for frying

  Tie in a muslin:
- 4 tsp fennel seeds
- 8 green cardamoms
- 5 cloves
- 2.5 cm stick of cinnamon
- 2 bay leaves

Batter
- 50 gm basmati rice
- 1 tsp powdered fennel seeds
- ½ tsp chilli powder
- 3 tbsp hung curd
- 50 gm flour
- salt to taste

Preparation

Wash the chicken and squeeze dry. Put the milk to boil in a large pan. Add the chicken pieces, spice bag, salt and saffron. Cook over a medium heat till the chicken is tender. Remove the chicken and keep aside. Squeeze the spice bag to extract maximum flavour and discard. Reserve stock.

Batter: Wash and soak the rice for an hour. Drain and grind finely alongwith the fennelseeds, chilli and salt. Beat the curd, add to the rice and gram flour. Add as much of the stock as needed to make a batter of pakoda consistency.

Heat enough oil in a karahi. Dip the chicken pieces in the batter. Let extra batter drip. Deep fry on a medium heat till a light brown. Remove and cool. You can prepare till this stage and refrigerate.

Just before serving, heat the oil once again and deep fry the tikkas till golden and crisp.

JAHANARI KABAB

Did Jahanara really eat this kabab or cook it? I'm not so sure, but the kabab surely is a good one, call it by any name.

Ingredients (Serves 6)

- 750 gm boneless chicken
- 1 large green capsicum
- 1 large red capsicum
- 2 large tomatoes
- 2 large onions
- 1 tbsp green chilli paste
- 2 tbsp mustard powder
- 1/3 cup lime juice
- salt and sugar to taste
- mustard oil for basting

Preparation

Cut the chicken in square pieces. Deseed and cut the capsicum the same way. Quarter the tomatoes and discard the seeds; divide each wedge into two. Quarter the onions and divide into sections with 2 petals each.

Mix the green chilli paste, mustard powder, lime juice, sugar and salt to taste. Rub the marinade well into the chicken and keep aside for 1 hour.

Skewer the chicken interspersed with the vegetables decoratively.

Grill over hot coals or in a tandoor or grill in the oven basting with a few drops of oil in between.

Serve with coriander chutney.

BEMISAL KABAB
(CHICKEN KABAB)

An unusual marinade that imparts sweet, sour and piquant flavours at the same time. Do make in large quantity or you will run of kababs.

Ingredients (Serves 6)
- 1 kg boneless chicken
- 1/3 cup honey
- 1 tbsp freshly ground pepper
- 1 tbsp chilli powder
- salt to taste
- 2 tbsp refined oil
- 1/3 cup thick tamarind pulp
- 1/3 cup tomato ketchup

Preparation
Cut the chicken in long thin pieces. Mix all the ingredients together and marinate the chicken in it for 1 hour.

Skewer the chicken from the middle as though you are running a needle through it. Use a thin skewer. Use 4–6 kababs per skewer depending on its size and pack tightly.

Cook in a tandoor, or grill in a hot oven or over coal fire, rotating and basting with the marinade till done.

Sprinkle lime juice over the kababs, if desired and serve at once.

Serve thinly sliced onions sprinkled with chaat masala and green chillies by the side.

FISH KABABS

MAHI KABAB AJWAINI
(FISH KABAB WITH AJWAIN)

Chaat masala did not feature in the original kababs. It's a very recent addition. But it imparts such a flavourful tang that I always enjoy its inclusion.

Ingredients

- ½ kg fish, cut into 1" (2.5 cm) boneless cubes
- 1 tbsp ginger–garlic paste each, juice of 1 lime
- 1½ tsp ajwain coarsely crushed
- ¼ tsp garam masala powder
- salt to taste
- 1 tsp chaat masala
- 1 tsp chilli powder
- 1 tsp cumin powder
- 1 tbsp refined oil

Preparation

Mix all the above ingredients and marinate the fish cubes in it for half an hour. Skewer and grill basting with butter.

Serve sprinkled with more chaat masala and lime juice, if desired, accompanied by a salad and a chutney.

SMOKED HILSA

A rather new fangled dish, but extremely popular with the young generation.

Ingredients

- 1.5 kg hilsa, whole
- 200 gm onion
- 100 gm ginger
- 1 tbsp kashmiri chilli powder
- 2 limes
- vinegar as required
- salt to taste

Preparation

Fillet the hilsa from both the sides in 2 large pieces. Your fish seller will do it for you. Cut the fillets vertically in 3 or 4 parts.

Marinate the fish in vinegar and salt for 7–8 hrs. Use vinegar generously. Take out from the vinegar and dry the fish with a towel. Now, if you press from one side you will be able to take out the large bones with your fingers easily or use a tweezer. Don't worry about the minute bones. They get dissolved.

Grind the onion and ginger without any water. Extract the juice. Mix with the lime juice and marinate the fillet in it for another 2 hours.

Grease a baking tray generously and lay the fish fillets side by side.

Preheat the oven to 200°C/400°F. Place a small aluminium container at the bottom of the oven. This should also be greased. Place 3–4 tbsp sugar in it.

Place the dish containing the fish on a rack just above the sugar. (You may brush the fish with a little tomato sauce and anchovy sauce at this point, if you want). Close the oven tightly.

A lot of smoke will generate and the flavour will penetrate the fish. Cook till done, turning once in between. Pierce with a needle to check. If it comes out clean, the fish is done.

PRAWNS WITH ORANGE MUSTARD SAUCE

This kabab tastes best if served with the following cucumber relish.

Ingredients (Serves 6)

- 12 tiger prawns
- 1½ tbsp soyabean sauce
- 1 tbsp sherry
- 2 tsp refined oil
- 1 tbsp cornflour, juice of 1 orange
- ½ tsp salt
- 1 tsp pepper

For Sauce

- 4 tbsp orange marmalade
- 2 tsp mustard paste
- 2 tbsp light soyabean sauce
- 2 tbsp orange juice
- 1 tsp lime juice
- ¼ tsp salt
- ¼ tsp pepper

For Relish

- 1 cup cucumber
- 1 small capsicum
- 1 small onion
- ¼ cup cooked prawns

For Dressing

- 3 tbsp lime juice
- 1 tsp chilli powder
- 1 tsp sesame seeds
- 1 tsp Thai fish sauce (optional)
- 1 tbsp sugar
- salt to taste

Preparation

Remove the heads, shell and delve in the prawns, keeping the tail tips on. Marinate in a mixture of soya sauce, sherry, oil, cornflour, orange juice, salt and pepper for 10 minutes.

Grill or bake for 6–7 minutes or till just done. Do not overcook. Remove and serve hot with the orange sauce.

Relish: Peel and finely chop the cucumber, onion and capsicum. Mix with the shrimps. Combine the dressing and pour over the relish. Chill and use.

Variation: Parcooked chicken or mutton nuggets can be used the same way. Or, grill or fry fish curbes and use.

Tandoori Fish

These delicately flavoured fish morsels are the pride of the table and just melt in the mouth as good tandoori kababs are supposed to.

Ingredients (Serves 6)

- 1 kg bhetki or surmai, cut into thick boneless cubes
- 1 egg
- 3 tbsp parched gram flour (Sattu)
- 1 tbsp ginger paste
- ½ tsp garam masala powder
- ½ tsp powdered mace
- ½ nutmeg, powdered
- 2 tsp allspice, powdered
- 1 tbsp coriander powder
- 1 tsp cumin powder
- 2 tbsp ghee
- 4 tbsp hung curd
- juice of 2 limes
- 1½ tbsp sugar, salt to taste
- 1 tbsp green chilli paste, a little butter

Preparation

Mix all the ingredients with the fish and marinate for 2 hours.

Pierce in skewers and cook in a tandoor or oven, basting with ghee till done aprx. 15 minutes. The sides of the fish should get slightly charred.

Place on a platter lined with lettuce leaves and pour hot melted butter on top and serve immediately.

Garnish with lime wedges and green chillies.

Chicken Reshmi Tikka

If you soak the chicken for only 2 hours, add 2 tbsp oil to the marinade. But long soaking always makes for succulent and soft kababs.

Ingredients (Serves 6)

- 700 gm boneless chicken, cut into small pieces
- 1 ½ tbsp lime juice
- 1 tsp salt
- ½ tsp chilli powder
- 1 tsp ginger garlic paste

Reshmi masala
- 3 tbsp refined oil
- 1 large onion, grated
- 2 cm piece of ginger, grated
- 4 green chillies, finely chopped
- 1 tbsp gram flour
- 1 tbsp cashewnut paste
- 1 tsp garam masala powder
- 1 tbsp chopped coriander leaves
- 1 egg
- ¼ cup hung curd

Preparation

Marinate the chicken with the lime juice, salt, chilli powder and ginger garlic paste overnight.

Reshmi masala: Heat the oil in a frying pan; fry the onion, ginger, green chilli till a light golden. Add the gram flour and stir till the raw smell disappears. Add cashew paste. Stir and remove from heat. Add garam masala powder and coriander leaves. Cool and add the egg, beaten. Apply the mixture on the chicken. Keep aside for 2 hours.

Put kababs thorugh skewers and place on an oven tray and grill the first side for 12 minutes, flip and grill for a further 8–10 minutes. Or, bake in preheated 400°F/200°C oven for 20–25 minutes or till tender.

You may prepare the kababs ahead of time. Just toss in hot butter before serving.

Variation: Hariyali kabab: add more coriander leaves and mint.

Kastoori Kabab: Add kasuri methi alongwith the marinade.

MAHI MAKHANI KABAB
(FISH BUTTER KABAB)

A marvellous kabab. As you cut into it, the butter oozes out to form its own sauce.

Ingredients (Makes 20 kababs)

- 150 gm butter
- 1 kg fish
- 2 large onions
- 25 gm ginger
- 4 cloves of garlic
- mustard or refined oil for frying
- 1 tsp turmeric
- 2 tsp chilli powder
- 1 tsp garam masala powder
- 4 green chillies, minced
- salt to taste
- 1 tsp sugar
- 1 bunch coriander leaves
- 6 slices bread
- 2 eggs
- dry breadcrumbs as needed

Preparation

Divide the butter into 20 equal parts and freeze.

Steam the fish. Debone and mash. Chop the onion finely. Grind ginger and garlic together. Chop the coriander leaves.

Heat 2 tsp oil in a karahi and fry the onion and ginger garlic paste till a light brown. Add the turmeric, chilli and garam masala powder and fry till golden brown. Remove from heat.

Mix this mixture with the fish alongwith the green chillis, coriander leaves, salt and sugar.

Dip the bread slices in water. Squeeze out the water and mash to a pulp. Mix to fish and knead the fish with your hands till smooth and all the ingredients are well mixed.

Divide into 20 equal portions. Roll each portion into a ball and stuff with a piece of frozen butter. Roll again and flatten slightly.

Beat the eggs, dip the kababs in the beaten egg, roll in breadcrumbs. Prepare all the kababs likewise. Refrigerate for half an hour.

Heat enough oil for deep frying in a Karahi. If using mustard oil, let it smoke, remove from heat, cool a little, then put on fire again. Fry the kababs, a few at a time till golden. Remove on an absorbent paper.

Serve hot with a salad and chutney.

Variation: Use finely ground chicken or mutton mince in place of fish. Boil mince, grind to a paste and proceed with the recipe.

A mix of boiled vegetables and paneer can be treated the same way.

Tandoori Pomfret

Ingredients (Serves 4)

- 4 pomfrets, about 400 gm–500 gm each

I. Marinade
- 100 ml malt vinegar
- 3 tbsp lime juice
- 2 tsp ginger paste
- 2 tsp garlic paste
- 1 tbsp green chilli paste
- salt to taste

II. Marinade
- 200 gm curd
- 1 egg
- 1 tbsp ginger paste
- 1 tbsp garlic paste
- 4 tbsp cream
- 2 tbsp gram flour
- 2 tsp ajwain
- 1 tsp white pepper
- 1 tsp chilli powder
- 1 tsp turmeric
- salt to taste

Preparation

Clean and wash the pomfrets, keeping them whole. Make 3 deep incisions across each side.

I. Marination: Mix all the ingredients together. Soak the fish in it for 1 hour.

II. Marination: Hang the curd tied in a muslin for 4 hours to let the whey drip off. Beat the curd and egg. Add the rest of the ingredients.

Take out the fish from the first marinade, shake off excess liquid. Rub the second marinade well into the fish, pushing inside the incisions. Keep aside for 2 hours.

Take 4 thick skewers and skewer the fish from mouth to tail. Roast in a tandoor for 5–7 minutes each side.

If you use an oven, keep a tray underneath to catch the drippings. Bake for 15 minutes. Turn once in between. Take out the fish, allow excess moisture to drip off.

Baste again with butter and roast for a further 3–4 minutes.

Serve with onion, cucumber and tomato slices and lime wedges.

JHINGA TIKKA
(PRAWN TIKKA)

I like to retain the heads of the prawns too. But that's upto you. If you retain the heads, clean them well. There's a small black bag in the head which must be removed.

Ingredients (Serves 6)

- 1 kg tiger prawns, after dressing

I. Marinade
- 3 tsp garlic paste
- 4 tsp ginger paste
- ½ tsp pepper
- ½ tsp chilli powder, juice of 1 lime
- salt to taste

II. Marinade
- 1 cup curd
- 1 tbsp ajwain
- 4 tbsp grated cheese
- 5 tbsp cream
- ½ tsp mace powder
- ½ tsp grated nutmeg
- 3 tbsp roasted chana dal powder (Salter)

Preparation

Shell the prawns, but retain the tail tips. Make a slit near the tail of each and carefully remove the veins. Clean the heads, but do not shell, if using.

I. Marination: Mix all the ingredients and soak the prawns in it for 30 minutes. Squeeze prawns gently to get rid of the moisture.

II. Marination: Hang the curd tied in muslin for 4 hours. Mix the hung curd with the rest of the ingredients and marinate the prawns in it for 30 minutes.

Use thin skewers. Skewer from the tail end in such a way that the whole prawn is pierced through. Use one skewer per prawn. This ensures that the prawns do not curl.

Place over medium heat for 10 minutes, brushing with marinade. Be careful not to overcook. Overcooking prawns make them dough.

FISH SEEKH KABAB

It's one of life's snack mysteries—putting food on a stick, improves the flavour.

Ingredients (Serves 6)

- 500 gm fish fillet
- 4 cloves
- 2 cm piece of cinnamon
- 1 black cardamom
- 5 peppercorns
- 1 tsp cuminseeds
- 5 cm piece of ginger
- 5 cloves of garlic
- 1 large onion, 2 green chillis
- 1 small bunch of coriander leaves
- 1 tsp chilli powder
- 2 tbsp gram flour
- 1 egg
- 1 tbsp amchur
- salt to taste
- 1 tbsp refined oil, onion petals, lime wedges and bay leaves as needed

Preparation

Process the fish fillets in a blender till minced to a smooth paste. Lightly roast and powder the cloves, cinnamon, cardamom, peppercorns and cuminseeds. Grind ginger and garlic. Very finely chop the onion, green chillis and coriander leaves.

Mix all the ingredients with your hands, kneading well. Divide the mixture into even sized balls. Roll balls onto skewers interspersed with onion petals, lime wedges and bay leaves.

Cook over live coals or grill in an oven basting with oil till well cooked.

Serve hot over a plate of saffron rice.

To make onion petals, quarter a large onion and separate each layer. While skewering, place 4 petals decoratively at a time.

Variation: The kababs may be skewered with baby onions, button mushrooms and cherry tomatoes.

Meat Kababs

Adrak Ke Panje
(Ginger Kababs)

Makes a very good side dish for any party.

Ingredients (Serves 6)
- 1 kg mutton chops with 2 riblets each
- 4 green cardamoms
- 5 cloves
- 1 small piece of cinnamon
- 10 pepper corns
- 2 tbsp poppy seeds
- 1½ tbsp mustard seeds
- 2 tbsp vinegar
- 2 tbsp ginger paste
- 1 tsp garlic paste
- 1 cup grape juice
- 1 tbsp sugar
- 1 large onion
- salt to taste
- 4 tbsp ghee
- 4 green chillies, chopped

Preparation

Wash and dry the chops. Grind the cardamoms, cloves, cinnamon, poppy seeds and mustard seeds together using vinegar instead of water (This vinegar is extra) to a smooth paste.

Mix the paste with vinegar, ginger–garlic paste, grape juice, sugar and salt. Marinate the chops in it for 2 hours.

Heat the ghee in a pressure cooker and fry the onions till golden. Add the green chilli and the marinated chops with the marinade. No water is to be added. Cook for 8 minutes.

Uncover and fry till the oil surfaces. Turn the chops gently in between once.

Alternatively the chops may be baked in an oven.

Garnish with grapes and fresh pomegranate seeds. Serve hot with parathas and naans.

PASANDA KABAB

A very specialised kabab par cooked and then baked. A pasanda is a lean meat fillet from the thigh portion, often made for special occasions. Your meat shop will prepare pasandas. for you. But if you can't get them made, compromise by beating boneless meat cubes into flat fillets– but it won't be the real thing.

Ingredients (Serves 4)

- 8 peppercorns
- 6 colves
- 2 cm cinnamon
- 4 red chillies
- 1 tbsp coriander seeds
- 2.5 cm piece of ginger
- 1 tbsp poppy seeds
- 1 tbsp chironji

- 1 tbsp magaj
- ½ cup hung curd salt to taste
- 2 tbsp ghee
- 500 gm meat pasandas or fillets
- 2 large onions, chopped, pinch of saffron
- 2-3 drops meetha itar

Preparation

Grind the pepper, cloves and cinnamon to a powder. Grind the red chillies, coriander and ginger to a paste. Separately grind the poppy seeds, chironji and magaj to a smooth paste.

Mix all the ground spices with half the curd and salt. Add half ghee. Soak the pasandas (beat them slightly at first) in it for 4 hours.

Heat the remaining ghee in a non-stick skillet. Add the chopped onion and saute till soft about 2 minutes. Add the meat and remaining curd and cook on a gentle heat. Add the saffron mixed with a little warm water. Stir meat twice in between.

When the meat is half cooked take out, cool and put on skewers. Finish cooking over a slow fire or in an oven.

Finally sprinkle the meetha itar and serve hot.

STEAMED KABAB

One doesn't always have the facility to grill or barbecue kababs. This recipe comes handy then.

Ingredients (Serves 6)

- 500 gm finely minced meat
- 1 large onion
- 2.5 cm ginger
- 4 cloves of garlic
- 4 green chillies
- ½ cup chopped coriander leaves
- 2 tbsp roasted gram,
- powdered or 1 egg
- ¼ tsp all spice powder
- ¼ tsp star anise, powdered
- 1 tsp coriander seeds
- 1 tsp cuminseeds
- 2 tsp aniseeds
- salt to taste

Preparation

Process the mince, onion, ginger, garlic, green chillies and coriander leaves together in the blender. Grind together the aniseed, coriander and cumin to a paste.

Mix the mince, onion, ginger, garlic, green chillies and coriander leaves together in the blender. Grind together the aniseed, coriander and cumin to a paste.

Mix the mince, roasted and powdered gram or the egg, ground spices, powdered spices and salt. Blend once again till well mixed.

Moisten your hands and roll on skewers like seekh kababs. Brush with oil.

Steam in a pressure cooker for 2–3 minutes; take out and fry in a non-stick skillet till golden.

Alternatively, lay the kababs gently side by side on a wide shallow pan. Put over a slow heat and cover pan for 5–10 minutes. Pour melted fat over the kababs and fry until golden brown.

Serve with a salad and coriander chutney.

NARGISI KABAB
(INDIAN SCOTCH EGG)

India's answer to British scotch eggs. Served with a robust salad and a spicy raita and preceeded by a soup, this constitutes a hearty mix and match meal.

Ingredients (Makes 10)

- 1 kg lean minced meat
- 2 large onions, chopped
- 1 cup Bengal gram dal
- 10 peppercorns
- 2.5 cm piece of cinnamon
- 6 green cardamoms
- 8 cloves
- 3 bay leaves
- 2.5 cm ginger
- 4 dry red chillies

- 3 cups of water
- ½ tsp garam masala powder
- ¼ cup mint leaves
- salt to taste
- 1 tbsp amchur
- 2–3 eggs
- flour as needed
- 10 hard boiled eggs, refined oil for frying

Preparation

Cook all the ingredients together except amchur, eggs, hardboiled eggs, flour and oil, and pressure cook for 10 minutes. Dry away any excess liquid. The mixture should be absolutely dry.

Grind on a grinding stone or a blender till well blended and smooth. Mix the amchur and raw eggs. Add 2 eggs to begin with, if you find the mixture stiff, only then add the other egg. Divide the mix in 10 equal parts.

Take 1 boiled egg, lightly coat with flour and then wrap the egg with one portion of the mince mix. Prepare all the kababs this way.

Heat enough oil in a karahi and deep fry the kababs till golden. Fry 2 at a time. Serve hot.

GANNE KA KABAB
(KABABS ON SUGARCANE)

An unusual kabab. The unusual part is that instead of the common skewers, sugarcane sticks are used imparting a fresh fruity flavour to the kababs.

To prepare the sticks, buy one whole sugarcane, divide into (18 cm 12") portions. Peel and cut each into 4 parts lengthways. The sugarcane seller will do this for you.

Ingredients (Serves 4)

- ½ kg minced meat
- 1 onion
- 1 tbsp coriander seeds
- 1 tsp cuminseeds
- salt to taste
- 8 red chillies
- 6 tbsp gram dal, juice of 1 lime
- 1 egg, ghee or oil as needed

Coarsely powder
- 2.5 cm piece of cinnamon
- ½ tsp grated nutmeg
- 4 petals of mace

Grind together
- 4 walnuts
- 1 tbsp Poppy seeds
- 10 chironji
- 2 tbsp magaj

Preparation

Boil the mince with the onion, coriander, cumin, salt, chilli and gram dal till done. Dry excess liquid, if any. Grind to a fine paste.

Add the lime juice, egg, powdered and ground ingredients and mix very well with your hands or blend in the processor.

Take the sugarcane sticks and wrap one part of the mince seekh kabab fashion. Brush with melted ghee or oil.

Roast in a tandoor or over live coals or grill in an oven rotating and basting with oil till golden and done.

DHUANWALI KABAB
(SMOKED KABAB)

Smoking meat this way is a part of the mughlai cuisine. A very easy way to impart a delicious smoky aroma to meats.

Ingredients (Serves 4)

- ½ kg minced meat
- 1 large onion, refined oil for frying
- 1 large bunch of fresh coriander
- 4 green chillies
- 1 tbsp ginger garlic paste
- 1 tbsp raw papaya paste
- ¼ cup hung curd
- 1 tsp pepper
- salt to taste
- ¼ tsp garam masala powder
- ¼ tsp kabab chini powder

Preparation

The mince must be ground very fine. Slice the onion evenly and thinly. Fry in oil till golden. Take out and spread on a piece of paper, so that the extra oil drains. This will become crisp, as it cools.

Mix the meat with all the ingredients with your hand till everything forms a mass. Make a space in the centre and place a live coal there. (If you take a piece of charcoal and put it over the gas, it will burn very easily).

Now, pour 1 tbsp ghee and 2 green cardamoms on the live coal and immediately cover the vessel. Keep covered for half an hour. The smokey flavour will penetrate the meat.

Discard the coal and cardamoms and mix the mince once again. Divide into lime sized balls and flatten into tikias.

Shallow fry in a non-stick skillet, a few at a time, till golden and well done.

Serve with a chutney.

BARA KABAB
(BAKED MUTTON CHOPS)

Juicy kababs with a spicy chatpata chutney are welcome anytime.

Ingredients (Serves 5–6)

- 50 gm raw papaya
- 50 gm ginger
- 50 gm garlic
- salt to taste, juice of 1 lime
- 250 gm curd
- 10–12 mutton chops (aprx. 1 kg)
- 2 tsp green chilli paste
- 1 tbsp kashmiri chilli powder
- 1 tsp cumin powder
- ½ tsp garam masala powder, mace, nutmeg and green cardamom powder–a pinch each
- 2 tbsp refined oil
- 2 tbsp ghee

Preparation

Grind the raw papaya. Grind the ginger and garlic together. The lamb chops should be cleaned of all fat and sinews. Rub in salt and lime juice. Next, rub well the raw papaya paste. Keep aside.

In the meantime, hang the curd tied in a muslin to drain whey. Beat the hung curd and add the rest of the ingredients. Marinate the chops in it for 4–6 hours. Longer marination helps the spices to penetrate the meat.

Grill the wire mesh of the gas tandoor and lay the chops, a few at a time and cover. Keep basting with oil. You will need 15 minutes per side, at least. See to it the meat gets well cooked. Turn once in between.

If you don't have a tandoor, bake for 40–45 minutes in a 200°C / 400°F oven, turning at least once.

KACHCHA KABAB
(SAUTEED KABAB)

If you have any reservation about using ghee or butter, use refined oil instead. But a mixture of ghee and butter gives best result.

Ingredients (Serves 6)

- 12 almonds
- 12 cashewnuts
- 20 raisins
- ½ kg minced meat
- 2.5 cm piece of ginger
- 6 cloves of garlic
- 4 green chillies
- 2 tbsp poppy seeds
- 6 small onions
- salt to taste
- 2 tbsp ghee
- 2 tbsp butter
- 1 tsp garam masala powder, pinch kabab chini powder

Preparation

Soak the almonds. Peel and grind alongwith the cashewnuts and raisins to a coarse paste. Set aside.

The mince must be lean. Grind ginger–garlic and green chillies together. Separately grind the poppy seeds.

Pressure cook the mince, onion, ginger–garlic, green chilli paste, poppy seed paste and salt with very little water for 10 minutes. Dry away excess liquid, if any. Grind the mince and mix with the almond paste.

Heat 1 tsp ghee and 1 tsp butter in a non-stick skillet. Put in the ground mince and spread evenly. Cook over medium high heat. When the underside turns brown, stir well and sprinkle a little of the ghee and butter and fry again.

Likewise, keep stirring and frying; add a little of the ghee and butter as you go on. Add the garam masala and kabab chini powder in between. The kabab should be well fried and somewhat crisp.

Serve hot with rotis or parathas.

Hussainy Kabab

Long marination makes for tender, juicy and succulent kababs. So marinate for as long as time permits, but do bring to room temparature before cooking.

Ingredients (Serves 4)
- 15 almonds
- 20 cashewnuts
- 2.5 cm piece of ginger
- 4 flakes of garlic
- 500 gm meat from the leg, with the bone removed and cubed
- salt to taste
- 1 tsp cumin powder
- salt and chilli powder to taste
- 4 tbsp butter
- ½ lt. milk
- 200 ml cream

Preparation
Blanch and peel the almonds and grind alongwith the cashewnuts to a paste. Separately grind ginger and garlic together. Mix salt, chilli, cumin and coriander powders to it and apply on top of the meat cubes. Mix well and set aside for a few hours. Grill, basting frequently with oil till tender and golden. Place in a serving dish.

Melt the butter. Add the milk, nuts and cream and cook over a slow fire till thick. Spread a thick layer of the cream mixture over each kabab. Serve at once.

↑ BOTI KABAB

← CHICKEN RESHMI TIKKA

FRUITY MUTTON TIKKA
↓

PASANDA KABAB
←

PEARL BALL →

PRAWN TIKKA
↓

CHUTNEY CHAAP
(MEAT RIBS WITH CHUTNEY)

A Kabab with a most refreshing fruity tang.

Ingredients (Serves 5–6)

- 1 kg meat chaap
- salt to taste
- 1 cup sweet fruit chutney
- ¼ cup chilli sauce
- 2 tbsp vinegar (preferably balsamic vinegar)
- 1 tbsp Worcestershire sauce
- 1 tsp mustard powder
- 1 tbsp minced onion
- ¼ tsp capsice sauce
- 1 kg of meat should yield 10 chaaps

Preparation

Add 1½ cups of water and pressure cook the chaaps for 8–10 minutes. Drain well. Sprinkle same salt.

Meanwhile, chop any large pieces of fruits, the chutney may have. Cook the chutney with the remaining ingredients and 1 tbsp water over medium heat till heated through.

Brush the chaaps with the sauce and grill for 10 minutes. Turn over, brush the sauce and cook for another 5–10 minutes.

Serve with a salad; a potato salad goes extremely well and pass the remaining chutney.

MEAT TIKKAS

Nothing is more inviting than the aroma of food cooking on an open fire.

Ingredients (Serves 4)
- ½ kg boneless meat, cut into 2.5 cm squares
- 1 tbsp ginger paste
- 1 tbsp garlic paste
- 1 tbsp lime juice
- salt and chilli powder to taste

Sauce
- 100 gm roasted groundnuts
- 1½ tbsp sesame seeds
- ½ cup thick tamarind juice
  ½ cup sugar or jaggery
- ½ tsp garam masala powder
- ½ tsp roasted and powdered cumin
- ½ tsp roasted and powdered coriander
- salt and chilli powder to taste

Preparation
Apply ginger, garlic, lime juice and salt to the meat cubes. You may also add 1 tbsp raw papaya juice to tenderise the meat. Let stand for a couple of hours.

Grill in an oven, or cook in a tandoor or barbecue the tikkas, skewered, till tender and golden. Baste with a little ghee or oil.

Put in a serving dish; pour the sauce over the tikkas and serve hot.

Sauce: Grind together the groundnuts and sesame seeds. Mix with the remaining sauce ingredients and cook over a slow fire till thick.

BOTI KABAB

Tender, juicy, spicy pieces of boneless mutton, charcoal grilled and served with bits of crisp vegetables. Ideal as a cocktail snack or for a barbecue.

Ingredients (Serves 6)

- 1 kg boneless meat, cut into 48 pieces
- 1 cup thick curd, 5 cm piece of ginger
- 8 cloves of garlic
- 2 tbsp lime juice
- 1 tbsp malt vinegar
- 6 dry red chillies, preferably kashmiri chillies
- 6 green cardamoms
- 2 black cardamoms
- 8 cloves
- 10 peppercorns
- 1 tbsp poppy seeds
- 1 tbsp chopped cashewnuts
- tbsp refined oil or ghee
- salt to taste

Preparation

Grind ginger and garlic together. Separately grind the chillies, poppy seeds and cashewnuts. Very lightly roast and powder the whole garam masalas. Blend everything with the curd.

Marinate the meat pieces in this mixture for 8-12 hours, arrange the lamb cubes on skeweres. Cook on a charcoal fire or in a rotisserie, till the lamb is tender. Keep basting with the marinade in between.

Serve hot, garnished with lemon slices, radishes and spring onions.

Sikandari Raan
(Whole Leg of Lamb)

The leftover raan makes excellent cold cuts. This travels well and also makes good picnic food.

Ingredients (Serves 10-12)

- 2 kg raan (leg of lamb)
- 75 gm ginger
- 75 gm garlic, 150 gm raw papaya
- salt to taste
- 2 tbsp chilli powder
- 750 gm thick curd
- 2 tbsp dry rose petals
- 150 ml refined oil
- 50 gm ghee, juice of 4 limes

Powder together
- 10 green cardamoms
- 5 black cardamoms
- 25 pepper corns
- 2 tbsp cuminseeds
- 2.5 pieces of cinnamon
- 15 cloves

Preparation

Wash and dry the raan, removing any visible fat. Prick all over with a fork or the sharp point of a knife. Grind the ginger, garlic and raw papaya together. Rub the raan with it alongwith 1 tbsp salt and half the chilli powder, keep aside.

Whip the curd and add the powdered masala, dry rose petals, 1 tbsp salt and the rest of the chilli powder. Add the oil and marinate the leg of lamb in it, rubbing the marinade well for at least 4 hours; preferably 24 hours in the refrigerator.

Take out 1 hour before baking. Place the raan alongwith the marinade in a roasting pan. Pour the melted ghee all over. You may also sprinkle 1 tbsp kewra water and 1 tbsp rose water if desired.

Preheat the oven to the highest mark, then turn down to 200°C/400° F. Put in the raan and bake for 1-1½ hours, basting with the marinade frequently till done. Take out and wait till cool enough to handle.

68

Cut into thick slices, pour the gravy on top. Sprinkle 2 tbsp powdered kasuri methi on top and the lime juice. Put in the oven for another 15 minutes and serve hot.

The sliced raan may be garnished with hardboiled eggs, lemon, cucumber, onion and tomato slices.

Sarson Ka Tikka
(Mustard flavoured kababs)

Always grind mustard seeds with a little poppy seed and a pinch of salt; salt draws the pungency of the paste while the poppy seeds help reduce the acidity that mustard generally aggravates.

Ingredients (Serves 6)
- ½ kg chicken nuggets or fish botis
- 2 tbsp black mustard seeds
- 1 tbsp yellow mustard seeds
- 4 green chillies
- 1 tbsp poppy seeds
- 1/3 cup hung curd
- 1 tsp chilli powder
- 2 tbsp mustard oil
- salt to taste

Preparation
Grind the mustard seeds, green chillies, poppy seeds and a pinch of salt together. Beat the curd and mix with the mustard paste and the remaining ingredients.

Apply all over the fish or chicken and let stand half an hour for the fish and an hour if chicken is being used.

String in skewers and barbecue or grill till done, basting with the marinade often.

You may skewer the fish or chicken alternating with pieces of green chilli or capsicum.

Serve hot with lemon wedges and a salad.

Dora Kabab

An interesting kabab for the sheer joy of unwinding the string which holds the delicate kabab.

Ingredients (Serves 6–8)

- 1 kg boneless meat
- 1 tbsp grated raw papaya
- 10 cm piece of ginger
- 2 tbsp freshly ground pepper
- 1 tbsp coriander powder
- ½ cup ghee
- 1 cup hung curd
- 2 tsp chilli powder
- salt to taste

Preparation

Trim the meat of excess fat. Pound the boneless meat pieces with a meat mallet or 'hamam dista' till reduced to a pulp. Add all the ingredients together and blend to a paste in the mixie.

Everything should be well mixed and very soft. Take a handful of the meat mixture and shape onto skewers like sheekh kababs.

Now, take ordinary thread and wrap around the kabab thoroughly.

Put in a tandoor, or barbecue or grill in an oven rotating and basting with ghee.

Serve with lime wedges. The guests will unwind the strings themselves.

LIVER KABAB

A kabab different from the one you have been used to.

Ingredients (Serves 6)

- 250 gm liver
- 1 tsp coriander powder
- 5 cm piece of cinnamon
- 5 cloves
- 3 green cardamoms
- 3 pieces of mace
- 5 cm piece of ginger
- 1 tsp freshly ground pepper
- 50 gm hung curd
- 50 gm butter
- salt to taste
- 1 lime

Preparation

Wash and cut the liver in medium square pieces. Do not wash the liver pieces thereafter.

Grind all the spices together. Beat the curd and mix in the ground spices, salt and pepper. Marinate the liver in it for 1 hour or longer, if time permits.

Thread onto skewers. Melt the butter; brush liver with it. Grill for 10 minutes, turning and basting often.

Sprinkle with the lime juice and serve hot with a salad.

These can also be shallow fried on a tawa. But take care not to overcook. Overcooking invariably makes the liver tough.

ROTI KABAB

Kababs accompanied by various breads have existed in many parts of the world but nobody thought of putting the two together to make a full meal. The idea of such a roll originated in Calcutta and is unique to this city. Nizam's, a restaurant in Calcutta, was the first to introduce this. Other establishments have copied the idea with varying degree of success, but Nizam's is still the best.

Ingredients (Serves 6)

Roti

- 2 cups flour
- ½ tsp baking powder, pinch of salt
- 1 tsp refined oil
- ½ cup milk, refined oil for frying

Kabab

- 300 gm boneless chicken nuggets
- 2 tbsp soyabean sauce
- 2 tbsp tomato puree
- 2 tsp ginger - garlic paste
- 1 tbsp thick curd
- ½ tsp salt
- ½ tsp freshly ground pepper
- 2 tbsp refined oil
- 100 ml coconut cream
- 2 tbsp roasted peanut powder, bamboo skewers

Preparation

Roti: Sieve the flour, baking powder and salt together. Rub in the oil and knead with the milk to a soft and smooth dough. Divide into a large lemon sized balls. Take each ball, roll into a thin rope and roll again into a coil. Prepare all the rolls this way. Smear the rolls with oil. Cover with a damp cloth and set aside till needed.

At the time of serving, roll each into a thin roti. Dry roast on a tawa and then drizzle just a little oil from the sides and fry. Do not let the rotis become crisp.

Take out the hot roti and place a few kababs in the centre and over it just a few slices of onions and green chilli. Sprinkle a little lime juice. Roll from one side while still hot. Wrap a paper napkin and serve hot, with a salad and chutney or ketchup.

Kabab: Soak the bamboo skewers in hot water 2 hours prior to using. This way they become piable and do not catch fire. To make coconut cream, grate a large coconut and take out 3 extractions of milk using 3 cups of hot water. Refrigerate this milk overnight. The cream will solidify on top. Take out and use.

Marinate the chicken nuggets in the above ingredients for 2 hours at least.

Pierce 6–8 pieces of chicken in each skewer. Roast over open fire rotating and basting till done. The nuggets cook quite quickly. Alternatively, grill in an oven.

Or, the chicken may be shallow fried on a tawa using very little oil. Use a non-stick tawa for ease in cooking.

Variation: Meat may be used the same way. Add 1 tbsp grated raw papya to the marinade.

Patila Kabab

So named because this kabab is invariably cooked in a patila or degchi.

Ingredients (Serves 4)

- 250 g minced meat
- 200 g onion
- 1 tsp ginger - garlic paste
- 1 tsp coriander powder
- ½ tsp garam masala powder
- 2 tbsp finely chopped fresh coriander
- salt to taste
- 1 tsp very finely chopped green chilli, ¾ cup refined oil
- 2 medium onions, cut into rings
- ¼ cup tomato ketchup
- 1 tbsp lime juice

Preparation

Grind the minced meat and onion separately. Mix minced meat, onion, ginger-garlic paste, coriander powder, garam masala, fresh coriander, salt and green chilli very well, use your hands to mix. Keep aside for 15 minutes. Shape like coctail sausages.

Heat the oil in a strong bottomed patila. Drop the kababs one by one carefully. Cover and cook over medium heat. The Kababs will release a lot of water, at first. Shake the patila often so the kababs cook evenly. Don't use a spoon. The water will evaporate and the kababs will be golden brown.

Drain excess oil and add the onion rings, tomato ketchup and lime juice. Cover and simmer for 10 minutes, carefully turning the kababs once. Toss and serve hot.

KHATTI MEETHI TIKKA
(SWEET SOUR NUGGETS)

If you're short of time, the mutton may be marinated for a shorter time. But the result won't be so soft and succulent.

Ingredients (Serves 6)
- 1 kg boneless meat, cut into bite sized cubes
- salt and pepper to taste
- 1 tbsp raw papaya juice
- 4 tbsp groundnut oil, finely grated rind and juice of 1 sweet lime
- 3 tbsp brown sugar
- 2 tbsp malt vinegar and tamarind juice
- 1 tbsp molasses
- 3 green chillies, finely chopped
- 2 tsp ginger paste
- 1 tsp capsico sauce

Preparation
Wash and dry the meat cubes thoroughly. Rub salt, pepper and papaya juice into the meat well. Combine rest of the ingredients and marinate the meat in it for 24 hours. Refrigerate and turn a few times in between. Let stand at room temperature for 1-2 hours before use.

Thread the pieces of meat onto shewers and barbecue over hot coals or use a tandoor or grill in an oven. Turn the skewers regularly to ensure even cooking and brush frequently with the marinade. Cook till done.

Garnish with onion, cucumber and lemon rings.

MINCE AND CHEESE KABAB

Instead of skewering, shape this delicious mixture into 12 tikias. Interleaved with grease proof paper they make a great freezer standby.

Ingredients (Makes 12)

- 4 large slices of bread
- 4 cubes Britannia cheese, grated
- 1 tbsp sweet mango chutney
- 1 onion finely chopped
- 350 g finely minced mutton or chicken
- 1 tsp ginger green chilli paste
- 1 tbsp refined oil
- salt and pepper to taste

Preparation

Remove the crusts and grind the bread slices into crumbs, grate the cheese. Chop the mangoes in the chutney very small. Mix all the ingredients together kneading well.

Divide the mixture and form into sausage shapes. Thread onto skewers.

Grill in a moderate oven, brushing with oil lightly. It will take about 20 minutes for mutton, less for chicken. Keep turning and brushing with oil off and on until cooked through.

Serve with a salad and chutney with roomali roti, naan or paratha.

Lagan Ke Kabab

One of Hyderabad's everlasting gifts to mankind is its cuisine. And this kabab is fine example. It derives its name from the special container, it's cooked in, called lagan.

Ingredients (Serves 6-8)

- 1 kg finely minced meat
- 2 tsp ginger paste
- 2 tsp garlic paste
- 1½ tsp raw papaya paste
- 2 tbsp lime juice
- 1½ tbsp refined oil
- salt to taste
- 50 ml curd, pinch of saffron
- 50 ml refined oil
- very lightly roast and powder : 2.5 cm stick cinnamon
- 4 cloves
- 2 blades of mace
- 5 green cardamoms
- 10 all spice

Preparation

Mash the mince, breaking all lumps. Add the ginger garlic paste, raw papaya paste, lime juice, salt, 1½ tbsp oil and the powdered masale. Mix, kneading well with your hands.

Take a 'Lagan' or a flat container and put some oil in it, taking care to spread it on all sides.

Make oval shaped kababs from the mince and place in the container. Do not overlap. Beat the curd and dissolve the saffron in it. Add a little curd on all the kababs. Sprinkle a little oil also.

Bake in a preheated 190° C/380° F oven for 25 minutes.

Garnish with onion rings and lime wedge.

Kakori Kabab
(Special Seekh Kabab)

The name comes from the place of its origin.
The texture of this kabab is far more smooth and tender than
the normal seekh kababas. They are best served with fragrant
saffron bread - sheermal.

Ingredients (Serves 6)

- 50 g raw papaya
- 1 large onion
- Refined oil for frying the onion
- 100 g gram flour
- 1 Kg minced mutton
- 250 g mutton fat, preferably from the kidneys
- Salt and chilli powder to taste
- Pinch of saffron, a few drops of kewra essence, ghee for basting
- Grind to a very smooth paste : 5 peppercorns 4 cloves
- 4 green cardamoms, 2 sticks cinnamon
- 2 tbsp poppy seeds
- 10-12 cashewnuts
- 150 g onions

Preparation

Grind the raw papaya to a fine paste. Finely slice the onions
and fry in oil, stirring till evenly golden. Remove onto an
absorbent paper. When cool, grind to a paste. Roast the
gram flour till fragrant.

Mince the mutton twice in the processor and a third
time with the fat.

Mix all the ingredients and the ground paste till you get
a smooth mixture. Knead well.

Make small balls of the mixture. Place this on thin
skewers about 10 cm in length. Place them 5 cm apart.

Cook over a charcoal fire or in a hot tandoor, basting
with ghee.

FRUITY MUTTON TIKKA

This is delicious on its own or as a rich beginning to a grand meal. For accompaniment you can use practically anything-sauce, chutney, cheese or wafer.

Ingredients (Serves 6)

- 700 gm boneless mutton, cut into 2.5 cm cubes
- 2 tbsp refined oil
- 3 tbsp Worcestershire sauce
- 1 tbsp coriander seeds, crushed
- 2 cloves of garlic crushed
- 8 bay leaves
- 1 large onion, 2 large magoes, juice of 1 orange
- 1 tsp lime juice
- 2 tbsp honey
- salt to taste

Preparation

The mutton must be bean. Mix together the oil, Worcestershire sauce, coriander, garlic and salt. Pour over the mutton. Toss well. Refrigerate 2 hours or longer, if possible.

Quarter the onion and divide into petals. Peel and discard the stone, cube the mango.

Drain the meat, reserving the marinade. Thread onto skewers interspersed with the bay leaves, (if the leaves are large, tear into two) onion petals and mango cubes.

Cook under a hot grill, tandoor. Or barbecue, turning a few times in between until the meat is tender, but simmer the leftover marinade with the orange juice, lemon juice and honey until it thickens and pour over the kabab.

Variation: Use peaches or pineapple in place of mangoes. Chicken may be used instead of mutton.

KAKORI KABAB

VEGETABLE KABAB

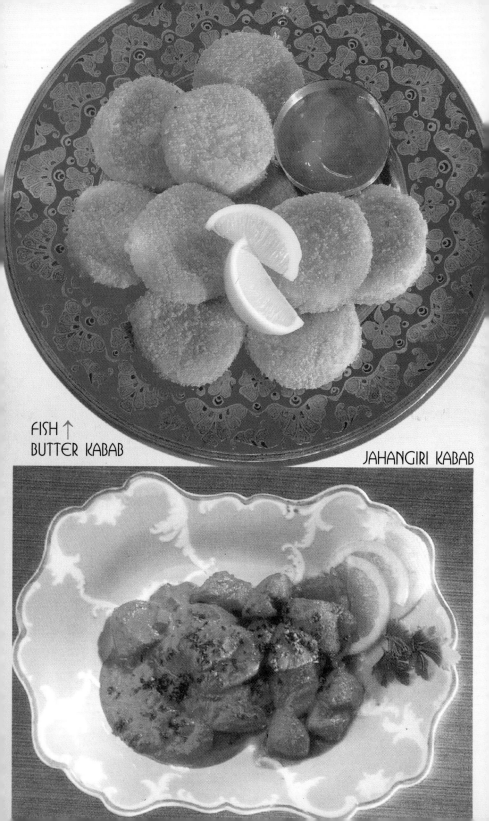

FISH ↑
BUTTER KABAB

JAHANGIRI KABAB

MASS KE SULE
(RAJASTHANI MUTTON KABAB)

This Rajasthani Kabab used to be made with game venison, quail, partridge etc. Now, of course, it's made with chicken, lamb or even paneer. I belive there are more than 10 ways of preparing the kababs; some exotic, some simple. Here is a method, that's somewhere in between.

Ingredients

- 500 gm boneless lamb cubes

I. Marinade
- Juice of 2 limes
- 1 tbsp ginger paste
- 1 tbsp garlic paste
- 2 tbsp raw papaya paste
- salt to taste

II. Marinade
- 1 tbsp chilli powder
- ½ cup cashewnut paste
- 1 tbsp ginger garlic paste
- 1 cup thick curd
- ½ cup brown onion paste
- 1 tbsp fresh coriander paste
- 2 tbsp refined oil or ghee

Preparation

I. Marination: Mix all the ingredients and rub into the lamb cubes. Keep aside for 2 hours.

II. Marination: To make the brown onion paste, thinly slice 2 medium onions, fry in oil over a medium heat, stirring constantly till golden. Take out on a piece of paper and when cooked, grind to a paste.

Beat the curd, add all the ingredients and marinate the meat in it for another 2 hours.

Skewer the lamb cubes at least 4 cm apart. Cook in a moderately hot tandoor or on live charcoal for 10-12 minutes. Can be grilled in an oven for 20 minutes.

Remove and hang the skewers to let extra moisture drip off. Baste with ghee and roast again for another 10 minutes or till tender.

Remove the cooked kababs onto a plate. Keep a small bowl in the centre. Place a live coal in it. Top with 4 cloves and paur 1 tbsp ghee on it. Quickly cover with a large lid. Keep thus for 5-10 minutes for the smoky flavour to permeate the kababs.

Uncover, remove kababs and serve hot.

SPICY SHAMI KABAB
(MINCED MUTTON AND DAL KABAB)

I think this is the best kabab ever. It's quick to cook, inexpensive and uncomplicated. Tastes good as cold as hot. Makes very good picnic and travel food. You can keep the kabab mixture refrigerated and ready. Fry the kababs when you happen to have guests.

Ingredients (Makes 25)

- 500 gm minced mutton
- 8 kidneys
- 8 tbsp Bengal gram dal
- 4 medicem onions
- 8 cloves of garlic
- 2.5 cm piece of ginger
- 10 peppercorns
- 2 black cardamoms
- 6 green cardamoms
- 1 tsp cuminseeds
- 4 dry red chillies
- 2 green chillies
- 5 cloves
- ¼ nutmeg
- 1 small stick cinnamon
- 1 blade of mace
- 4 tbsp coriander leaves
- 2 eggs
- 8 almonds
- 8 cashewnuts
- 12 raisins
- salt to taste
- Juice of 1 lime
- Ghee or oil for frying

Preparation

Trim the kidneys of all fats. Soak the dal for 1 hour. Blanch the almonds. Skin and chop the almonds, cashewnuts and raisins.

Pressure cook all the ingredients together except the eggs, almond, cashewnuts, raisins, lime juice and ghee with 1 cup of water for 10 minutes. Open cooker and dry excess moisture, if any.

Grind the mince either in the blender or on a grinding stone till smooth. Do not add water. See to it that the spice are well blended with the mince.

Add the eggs and lime juice. Knead well. Divide into 25 equal sized balls. Place a little of the nut mixture in each.

Flatten each ball to shape like a tikkia. It helps if you work with moistened hands.

Fry on a non-stick tawa spreading ghee by the sides. Fry a few kababs at a time. These can be deep fried also.

Serve with a chutney.

KACHCHE AAM KA KABAB
(SKEWERED MUTTON WITH
GREEN MANGOES)

Foodies have a rare treat in store for them when served with this unusual sweet and tangy kabab.

750 gm boneless mutton or chicken, cut into 2.5 cm cubes, a few drops of ghee or oil for basting.

Ingredients (Serves 6)

I. Marinade
- 1 tbsp raw papaya paste with skin, juice of 1 lime

II. Marinade
- 1 green mango, peeled and grated
- 2.5 cm piece of ginger
- 4 green chillies
- 1 cup cream
- 10-12 mint leaves
- salt
- 1 tsp white pepper

Preparation

I. Marination: Mix the raw papya paste and lime juice and rub the mixture all over the mutton cubes. Keep aside for 1 hour.

II. Marination: Blend together the mango, ginger, green chilli and mint. Whop the cream and mix the salt, white pepper and the ground paste.

Now, shake off as much of the papaya paste as you can from the meat and marinate with the green mango mixture for at least 2 hours, longer, if time permits.

If you're using chicken, you may omit the first marinade altogether because chicken cooks quite quickly, anyway.

Thread the meat pieces on skewers and grill. You may use a tandoor or oven or hot coals. Keep turning and basting with the marinade and ghee, rotating till done.

Serve with cucumber and onion cut into rings, green chillies and lime wedges.

Malai Kabab
(Kabab with Cream)

Ingredients (Serves 4)
- 1 slice of bread
- 250 gm minced mutton
- 1 small onion, finely chopped
- salt to taste
- ¼ cup finely chopped coriander leaves
- 1 tsp kasoori methi powder
- 1 egg
- ½ cup cornflour, refined oil for frying
- 125 ml cream

Preparation

Grind the bread slice to crumbs. Grind the minced meat well. Add the onion, ginger, green chilli, salt, coriander leaves, kasoori methi powder and mix, kneading well. You may also blend very friefly in the mixie.

Add the breadcrumbs and egg; knead well again. Divide the mixture into 8–10 parts. Shape into tikias and coat with the cornflour. Shake off excess.

Shallow fry both the sides till lightly coloured about 5 minutes. Remove. You'll have to do this in two batches.

Put in an ovenproof dish. Pour the cream on top. Sprinkle a little chilli powder and the Kasuri methi.

Bake in preheated 350°F/ 180°C oven for 20 minutes or till a crust is formed.

Serve hot with a salad.

Dahi Kabab
(Kababs in Curd)

The kababs may be made a day or two ahead; your pre-party work will be easier.

Ingredients (Serves 6–8)

- 1/2 kg keema
- 115 gm Bengal gram dal
- salt to taste
- 1 tsp chilli powder
- 1 large onion, roughly chopped
- 2.5 cm piece of ginger
- 4 tbsp hung curd
- 1 tsp garam masala powder
- 1 egg, a pich of powdered mace, a pich of green cardamom powder, refined oil for frying

Stuffing
- 1 large onion, very finely chopped
- 4 green chillies, finely chopped
- 2 tbsp fresh coriander and mint each, chopped

Curd
- 2 cups thick curd
- 1 tsp chilli powder
- 2 tsp roasted and powdered cumin, black salt to taste

Preparation

Sweet tamarind chutney as needed. Use green chillies and fresh coriander for garnishing.

Boil the minced meat, gram dal, salt, chilli powder, onion and ginger till done. Evaporate excess moisture, if any. Grind in the mixie alongwith the remaining ingredients. The mixture should be very tight.

Divide into lime sized balls. Stuff with a little of the stuffing ingredients mixed together. Shape like tikias and shallow fry in hot oil on a tawa till golden. Let cool.

Curd: Whip the curd till smooth. Add all the other ingredients (may add 1 tbsp sugar) and beat once more.

To Serve: Place two kababs on each plate. Cover generously with the curd and sprinkle 1 tbsp tamarind chutney on top. Garnish with fresh coriander and green chillies.

These taste equally good when chilled.

KALI MIRCH KA KABAB
(PEPPER KABAB)

This extremely tasty kabab requires incredibly few ingredients.

Ingredients (Serves 6)

- 10-12 meat chops, aprx.
- 1 kg 50 gm peppercorns, juice of 2 limes
- 2 tbsp raw papaya juice
- 2 tbsp ginger juice
- 4 tbsp onion juice
- salt to taste, malt vinegar as needed
- 2 tbsp refined oil

Preparation:

Clean the chops of all visible fats and sinews. Gently pound the chops a little. Coarsely crush the peppercorns.

To make raw papaya juice, grate 1 papaya with the skin and squeeze to obtain the juice.

Soak the chops in all the juices and salt. Add vinegar generously so that they are well coated. Keep refrigerated for at least 24 hours turning a few times in between.

Take the chops out of the marinade. Squeeze gently to get rid of excess moisture. Press the crushed pepper on both the sides. There should be a thick coating. Drizzle each chop with a few drops of oil.

Cook in a hot tandoor or in an oven (200°C/400° F) for 15 minutes or till done.

Serve with a salad and a raita.

NAWABI KABAB

It's best if you buy the meat and mince at home, otherwise, blend the minced meat once again after buying.

Ingredients (Serves 6)

- 500 gm minced meat
- 2 slices of bread
- 4 medium onion, minced
- 4 green chillies, very finely chopped
- 1 tbsp grated ginger
- ½ cup chopped fresh coriander salt to taste
- 1 tsp chilli powder
- 1 tsp pepper
- 1 tsp cumin powder
- 1 tsp coriander powder
- ½ tsp garam masala powder
- 2 eggs
- ½ cup cornflour, refined oil for frying
- 200 ml cream

Preparation

Discard the crusts of the bread, soak in milk and squeeze dry. Mix the mince, breadcrumbs, onion (squeeze to get rid of moisture), green chilli, ginger, fresh coriander, salt chilli powder, pepper, cumin, coriander and half of the garam masala. Knead with your hands well till thoroughly combined. Add the eggs a little at a time. Add as much eggs as the mince can take without getting soggy.

Divide the mince into 18–20 portions, shape into round kababs. Dredge each kabab with cornflour. Shake off excess.

Heat oil in a skillet and fry a few kababs at a time till golden.

Place the kababs in an ovenproof dish. Pour the cream over it. Sprinkle a little salt, chilli powder and the remaining garam masala.

Bake in an oven preheated to 200°C/400° F for 20-30 minutes or till thick.

Alternatively, place the kababs in a flat vessel and pour the cream. Cook over a medium heat till thick.

Garnish with fresh coriander and green chillies.

DILKHUSH KABAB

Ingredients (Serves 6)

- ½ kg minced meat
- 2.5 cm piece of ginger
- 2 green chillies
- ½ coconut, a handful of grated, chopped fresh coriander
- 1 tbsp parched gram flour (sattu)
- 2 eggs
- ½ tsp garam masala powder
- 2 tsp coriander powder
- salt to taste
- 4 tbsp refined oil
- 2 bay leaves
- 4 cloves
- 2 green cardamoms
- 2 sticks cinnamon

Preparation

The mince should be ground very fine. Grind together the ginger, green chilli and coconut.

Mix mince and all the ingredients together except oil, bay leaves and garam masala. Mix extremely well using your hands.

Heat the oil in a skillet, non-stick preferred. Temper with the whole garam masala, slightly crushed. When they change colour, add 4 cups of water. Let it come to a boil.

Smear some oil on your palms and make small balls of the mince mixture. Flatten a little and drop carefully into the boiling water. When all the balls are thus immersed, cover and let cook for 20-25 minutes or till the water dries completely. Uncover for the last 10 minutes. Shake the pan occasionally.

When the water evaporates and the oil comes out, carefully turn the kababs once and let fry to a golden brown.

Serve hot with a chutney and raita.

Lemon Grass Kabab

Cooking would be a lot less fun if it wasn't for the kababs. The flavour and aroma of lemon grass make it an excellent companion for meat. So, let the herb work its magic in the kabab.

Ingredients (Serves 4)

- 100 gm fresh bread crumbs
- 500 gm minced meat
- 1 tbsp thick tomato puree
- 1 egg
- 1 tbsp Thai fish sauce or soyabean sauce
- 1 large onion, finely chopped
- salt and pepper to taste
- 4 tbsp minced lemon grass, white part only, sticks of lemon grass, refined oil as needed

Preparation

Combine all the ingredients together, except the lemon grass and lemon grass sticks. With moistened hands form into 12 balls. Then roll them in finely minced lemon grass.

Thread onto the lemon grass sticks. Brush with oil. Grill or barbecue for 15–20 minutes, turning frequently and brushing with oil until well browned.

Serve with barbecue or tomato sauce on a bread of rice and with a fresh green salad.

Variation: Fresh rosemary and rosemary sticks work very well the same way.

BAIDA KABAB
(EGG KABAB)

Ingredients (Serves 4)

- 1 tsp grated ginger
- 2 cloves of garlic
- 2 green chillies, refined oil for deep frying
- 1 medium onion
- 1 large tomato
- salt to taste
- ½ tsp sugar
- 4 hardboiled eggs
- 1 egg
- 1 cup fresh bread crumbs
- ½ cup chopped coriander leaves

Preparation

Grind the ginger, garlic and green chillies together. Finely chop the onion and tomatoes.

Heat 1 tbsp oil in a frying pan. Add the onion; stir fry. Add the tomato and the ground paste. Fry till the tomato is cooked and well mixed. Add the salt, sugar and fresh coriander.

Grate the hardboiled eggs. Add to the masala and mix well. Spread in a plate evenly and refrigerate for 4 hours.

Cut into long strips, like finger chips. Dip in the beaten egg and coat with the breadcrumbs. Deep fry in hot oil till golden.

Serve with a salad or chutney.

KABABS FROM FAR AND NEAR

What's in a name ? Kababs by any other name will taste just as delicious. What we know as kababs in India is called kabob, shish kabab,barbecue, grills in other lands. And all the world loves a kabab.

The happy news is that the exotic ingredients like jalapeno chillies, balsamic vineger, naam pla (Thai fish sauce), different herbs, exotic fruits and vegetable etc. are all available in our country these days. I've also given substitutes in case you can't procure the real thing. The taste may vary a little, but will still be very good.

JERK CHICKEN

A kabab from Jamaica - West Indies.

Ingredients
- 8 regular pieces of chicken
- 1 bunch spring onion, white part only
- 2 green chillies
- 5 cm piece of ginger
- 1 clove of garlic
- 2 dry chillies
- ¼ tsp all spice powder
- 1 cm stick of cinnamon
- 2 cloves, 4 tbsp soya bean sauce
- 2 tbsp malt vinegar, salt and pepper to taste

Preparation
Rinse the chicken pieces and pat dry with absorbent paper. Place in a shallow dish.

Grind the spring onion, green chillies, ginger, garlic, dry chillies, all spice, cinnamon and cloves to a smooth paste. Mix this paste with the soya sauce, vinegar, salt and pepper.

Pour mixture over chicken. Turn chicken portions over to coat thoroughly in the marinade. Refrigerate, cover, for up to 24 hours or as time permits.

Remove chicken from the marinade and barbecue or grill or cook in a tandoor for 30 minutes, turning the chicken over and basting occasionally until the chicken is cooked through. Serve at once with mango salsa.

MANGO SALSA

Ingredients

- 2 large firm ripe mangoes
- 2 kiwi fruits
- 2 red table radishes
- ¼ cup mango juice
- 1 spring onion
- ¼ tsp salt
- 1 tbsp lime juice
- 1 tbsp sugar
- 1 green chilli

Preparation

Peel and dice the mango and kiwi fruits. Finely dice the radishes. Very finely chop the spring onion and green chilli. Combine all the ingredients. Cover and refrigerate till needed.

Sausage, Bacon and Kidney Kabab

The scope of a kabab is very wide and this one has an unusual mixture of ingredients. The quick barbecue sauce is useful for basting and serving with most kind of kababs.

Ingredients (Makes 6 Kababs)

- 12 spicy sausages
- 12 kidneys
- 6 rashers streaky bacon
  Quick barbecue sauce:
- 4 tbsp tomato ketckup
- 2 tbsp sweet and hot sauce
- 2 tbsp refined oil
- salt and pepper to taste

Preparation

Cook the sausages for 10 minutes. Drain. Halve each sausage. Take the transparent skin off the kidneys, then cut them in half by length and with a very sharp knife cut out the centre core. Cut the rind of the bacon with a pair of kitchen scissors.

Thread the skewers with sausages halves, kidneys halves and bacon alternating under and over them.

Grill, rotating for about 20–25 minutes, brushing them occasionally with the barbecue sauce.

Serve the kabab on rice. Heat the rest of the sauce and serve it separately.

Barbecue sauce: Mix all the ingredients together and serve.

KIBBEH ON SKEWERS
(LEBANESE KABAB)

Kibbeh, a mixture of minced meat and dalia is a national dish of Lebanon. Preparing and eating kibbeh is not only a hallowed tradition; it is a countrywide addiction. It is made in a number of ways. This is cooked like a kabab. Now, you can make your own kibbeh at home.

Ingredients (Serves 4–6)
- 200 gm dalia (broken wheat)
- 500 gm minced meat
- 1 large onion, finely chopped
- ½ tsp all spice powder
- ¼ tsp cinnamon powder
- ¼ tsp grated nutmeg
- 1 tsp chilli powder
- salt and pepper to taste

Preparation
The mince should be very lean, preferably from the hind legs and very finely minced. Mince it once again at home. Soak the broken wheat for an hour in hot water and drain. Squeeze to dry very well.

Finely chop the onion and mix the mince, the cinnamon, all spice powder, nutmeg, chilli, salt and pepper.

Moistening your hands now and then by dipping them into a bowl of lightly salted iced water, knead the mixture until well blended and smooth. For a finer consistency, You may mince the mixture once again adding a tbsp of iced water.

Moistening your hands, take about 3 tbsp of the mixture, form it into a sausage shape and flatten slightly. Thread each one onto a bamboo skewer (presoaked in water to prevent scorching).

Roast the kibbeh under a hot grill or over live coals until golden brown and cooked through. Serve with a curd sauce.

CHINESE BARBECUED LAMB

The marinade for the meat also makes a very good dip to serve with this kabab or any other for that matter. Bring to a boil before serving. Do not use the tea leaves in that case.

Ingredients (Serves 6)

- 1 tbsp tea leaves
- ½ cup sesame seed paste
- 3 tbsp soya bean sauce
- 1½ tsp malt vinegar
- 1½ tbsp sesame oil
- 1 tbsp chilli oil
- 1½ tbsp sugar
- 2 spring onions, chopped
- 2 cloves of gralic, minced
- 750 gm cubed boneless meat, salt to taste

Preparation

To make chilli oil : Heat 1 cup refined oil till smoking. Take off heat. Wait 5 secs and then add 2 tbsp chilli powder. It will sizzle. Cover and let cool. Strain into a clean botttle. Refrigerated, it will keep for 4–6 months. Outside, for at least 6–8 weeks.

Parboil meat in pressure cooker for 5 minutes. Drain well and prick each with fork.

Steep the tea leaves in 3/4 cup boiling water. Strain to measure 1/2 cup. Discard tea leaves.

Combine tea liquor and the rest of the ingredients and meat; stir to mix well. Refrigerate for 4–6 hours.

Place 4–5 cubes of lamb on each skewer an inch apart.

Grill in an oven or cook in tandoor or barbecue on open fire, turning frequently and basting with the marinade.

Hawain Meat Brochettes

Did you know that meat with pineapple is not just a matter of taste ? Fresh pineapple (not tinned) contains bromelin, and enzyme which naturally tenderises meat. After a few hours marinating in the fresh juice even potentially tough cuts end up tender and succulent.

Ingredients (Serves 6-8)

- 1 kg boneless meat, cut in ribbon like long pieces
- 1 green, 1 yellow and 1 red capsicum
- 1 pineapple, few cherry tomatoes, 12 mushrooms

Marinade

- 1 ½ cups fresh pineapple juice
- 1 tsp capsico sauce
- 1 tbsp balsamic vinegar
- 1 tbsp honey
- 1 tsp chilli sauce
- salt and pepper to taste

Preparation

Mix the marinade ingredients together. Soak the meat pieces in it for as long as time permits.

Deseed and cut the capsicums in square pieces. Peel and core the pineapple and cut into cubes. Keep the mushrooms and tomatoes whole. You may use tinned pineapple.

Pierce the vegetables and pineapple through skewers. In separate skewers, thread the meat pieces.

Grill both the meat brochettes and vegetable skewers, basting with the marinade till the meat is done and the vegetables get charred by the sides.

Place both the skewers on a platter lined with lettuce leaves.

ARABIAN KABAB

The meat should be absolutely lean. That is the success of this kabab.

Ingredients (Makes 25 small kababs)
- ½ kg chops from the ribs (seene ka chaap)
- 1 cup milk
- 1 onion
- 1 boiled potato
- 1 cube of cheese, grated
- ½ tsp pepper powder
- chopped fresh coriander, green chillies and salt to taste
- 1 egg dry breadcrumbs as needed, refined oil for deep frying

Preparation
Cook the ribs in a pressure cooker alongwith the milk and onion for 10 minutes. The meat should be thoroughly tender and dry. Evaporate excess moisture, if any.

Cool and remove the meat from the bones but save the bones for later use.

Grind the meat alongwith the onion in a mixie or pound in a 'hamam dista' (mortar and pestle). Now, add the boiled potato, cheese, pepper, coriander leaves, green chillis, salt and mix well.

Form small balls from this mixture, sticking one bone in each ball and form into lollipops.

Beat the egg. Dip the kababs coating them well. Roll in crumbs. Deep fry in hot oil till golden.

MEAT AND VEGETABLE SHISH* KABAB

For an authentic Middle Eastern meal serve these delicious kababs with Tabbouleh (dalia salad), cucumber dip and warm pita bread.

Ingredients (Serves 6–8)

Meat
- 1½ kg boneless meat cubes

Vegetables
- 12 small firm red tomatoes
- 1 capsicum
- 12 button mushrooms
- 1 medium brinjal
- 12 small onions

Marinade
- 1 cup olive oil or refined oil
- 1/3 cup lime juice
- 2 garlic cloves, very finely chopped
- 1 tsp salt
- 1 tsp freshly ground black pepper
- 1 tbsp grated ginger

Preparation

Meat: The meat should be lean; cut into 1½–2 inch cubes.

Vegetables: Deseed and cut the capsicum into square pieces. Cube the brinjal into 12 cubes. Peel and parboil the whole onions 5–10 minutes or until barely tender.

Marinade: Combine all the ingredients. Add to the meat and marinate for at least 2 hours, turning frequently or upto 24 hours in the refrigerator.

To cook: Take long skewers; pierce the meat and vegetables. Leave a little space between meat cubes so that they cook well.

Grill over hot coals or in an oven or in a tandoor. Brush with the marinade and turn frequently. Cook till done. The kababs will continue to cook a bit off the flame, so be careful not to overcook them.

---

* This variety of Kabab is popular in Middle-east which is known as Shish Kabab

KEBALE

A Kabab from Yugoslavia, with a distinctive taste.

Ingredients (Serves 6-8)
- 24 cocktail sausages
- 750 gm cooked ham, cut into cubes

Glaze
- 2/3 cup fresh fruit chutney
- 1/3 cup mild mustard
- 1/3 cup malt vinegar
- 1 tbsp honey
- salt and freshly ground pepper to taste

Preparation
Parboil the sausages. Pierce the sausages and ham cubes alternately in skewers.

Glaze: Blend all the ingredients in a bowl until smooth, adding a little water, if necessary for a spreadable consistency.

With a brush, evenly spread the glaze all over the meat. Grill over hot coals or in an oven, turning and brushing with the glaze frequently for 8 - 10 minutes.

Serve hot.

CHICKEN SATAY

When it comes to kababs, variety is the spice of life. The satay is cooked and served all over the Far East, Thailand, Malaysia, Indonesia. Next time you host a kabab party let this be your centre piece.

Ingredients (Serves 6–8)

- 1 kg boneless chicken cubes
- 1 tsp coriander seeds
- 1 tsp cuminseeds
- 2 stalks lemon grass
- 2 tbsp roasted peanuts
- salt to taste
- 1 tsp sugar
- 1 tsp powdered cinnamon
- 2 tbsp fish sauce
- 1 tbsp refined oil
- 2 spring onions, white part only, chopped, a few spring onion bulbs, a few stalks lemon grass
- ½ cup thick coconut milk

Peanut sauce
- 1 cup jaggery or brown sugar
- 1 onion
- ½ cup tamarind paste
- 2 stalks lemon grass
- 2.5 cm ginger
- 3 tbsp crushed dry red chillis
- 300 gm roasted peanuts
- salt to taste
- 1 tbsp refined oil
- 1 cup thick coconut milk
- 1 tbsp fish sauce

Preparation

Grind the coriander, cuminseeds, peanuts, lemon grass, salt and sugar. Mix the ground paste with cinnamon, fish sauce, 1 tbsp oil spring onions and coconut milk. Marinate the chicken with this mixture for a couple of hours.

Skewer 5 cubes of meat on one skewer, as in kabab. Place two stalks of lemon grass in between and one spring onion bulb at the beginning and end of each skewer. Grill over live coals or in an oven, constantly brushing oil over the meat, using crushed lemon grass. Turn over and continue grilling until chicken is cooked. Serve with peanut sauce.

Peanut Sauce: Grind the peanuts. Keep aside. Grind lemon grass and ginger together. Slice onion. Heat the oil in a karahi. Add sliced onion and fry till soft. Add the crushed chillies and ground spice. Stir fry for 2 minutes. Add in tamarind juice, jaggery or brown sugar, salt, peanuts, coconut milk and fish sauce. Simmer till thick.

To serve: Arrange the sticks of satay on a plate and serve with the peanut sauce, sliced cucumber and onion. Served with a rice dish, it makes a full meal.

The fish sauce may be replaced by soya bean sauce.

FRUIT KABAB

Fruit Kababs can be classified as desserts. But they also make a very interesting change accompanied by rice or served alongwith other kababs.

Ingredients (Makes 8)

- 1 small pineapple
- 1 apple
- 2 kiwi fruits
- 24 large strawberries
- 24 cherries, fresh or tinned

For Dressing

- 1 tbsp lime juice
- 2 tbsp orange juice
- 1 tbsp honey
- 1 tbsp orange rind, grated
- 1 tsp grated lime rind
- 8 skewers

Preparation

Peel and core pineapple, cut into 2.5 cm (1") cubes. Peel and quarter kiwi fruits. Core, but do not peel the apple; cut into 8 pieces, stone cherries. Thread fruits alternately onto skewers.

Dressing: Combine all ingredients in small bowl. Beat well. Brush skewers with orange dressing.

Cook over gas flame, turning frequently. Baste with the dressing while cooking. Or, grill in a hot oven or barbecue.

Use any other fruit of your choice like honeydew melon (kharbuja), papaya, mango etc.

SWEET KABAB

A dessert kabab from the land of the Big Apple. This colourful kabab alternates fresh fruits and is just the thing for children's parties.

Ingredients

- Apple, banana, pineapple, fresh or canned; water melon, honeydew melon, papaya, mango, kiwi fruit, star fruit, guava

Choco sauce
- $1/_3$ cup cocoa powder
- 1 cup sugar
- ¼ tsp salt
- 1 cup of water
- ¼ tsp vanilla

Preparation

Use whatever fruit you can get. Peel and cut fruits into bite sized chunks, slices or shapes (use cookie cutter or melon baller).

To make one kabab, carefully push a thin skewer through the fruits, alternating colours and shapes. For a sweeter one, you may use marshmallows, too. Toast the kababs very lightly, if wished.

Dip in chocolate sauce, sprinkle with nuts and serve. May be chilled and served also.

Choco sauce: Mix cocoa powder, sugar, salt and water. Cook over medium heat until syrupy. Remove and add vanilla.

You may add 1/4 cup chopped milk or bitter chocolate or a combination of both. Thin down with water to the desired consistency.

These kababs can be made savoury, too. Sprinkle chaat masala, lime juice, and dip in a sweet sour tamarind chutney or a hot barbecue sauce.

Dessert Kabab

There are some kababs which can be served as desserts making them ideal for barbecue parties.

Ingredients (Serves 4)

- 4 bananas
- 16 cake pieces
- 4 tbsp jam
- 4 tbsp dessicated coconut
- 2/3 cups brown sugar
- ½ tsp cinnamon powder
- 2 tbsp lime juice, Ice cream to serve

Preparation

Bananas should be ripe but firm. Peel and cut into thick chunks. The cake should be cut in cubes.

Whip the jam and brush the cake pieces with it. Roll in dessicated coconut.

Mix the brown sugar and cinnamon powder. Brush the bananas with lime juice and roll in brown sugar.

Thread bananas and cakes alternately onto skewers. Toast over hot coals or under the grill till hot and aromatic.

Serve topped with ice cream at once.

Use any other firm fruits like pear, apple, peach, apricot.

ACCOMPANIMENTS

Kababs won't taste half as good without an accompanying dip or sauce or chutney. So here go a few. Some of the sauces and chutneys can also double up as marinades.
Sweet sour Tamarind chutney.

Ingredients

- 100 gm dates
- 50 gm munakka (seeded) or raisins
- 2 lime sized balls of tamarind
- ½ tsp dry ginger powder
- ½ tsp chilli powder
- ½ tsp pepper, 1 tsp roasted and powdered cumin, black salt and sugar to taste

Preparation

Soak the dates and munakka overnight. Pressure cook with 1 cup of water and tamarind for 10 minutes. Let it cool. Blend in a mixie and strain.

Put all the remaining ingredients and the strained mixture alongwith 1 cup of sugar. Let cook on a medium fire till thick like ketchup. Taste and adjust sugar and seasonings.

Refrigerated, this chutney keeps well for at least a month. So it's worthwhile making at least double the quantity.

Pesto Dip

Pesto dip actually uses basil leaves. I have Indianised it by using fresh coriander leaves. You may add a few mint leaves also.

Ingredients (Makes 2 cups)

- 2 cups packed coriander leaves
- 1/4 cup grated cheese
- 1 clove garlic, minced
- ¼ tsp salt
- ½ tsp freshly ground pepper
- 1 cup thick curd
- 3/4 cup cream

Preparation

In food processor, combine coriander leaves, cheese, garlic, salt and pepper. Process, using on off pulses, until minced, scraping down sides of bowl with rubber spatula once or twice.

Add the curd and cream; pulse until just evenly combined. Pour into a bowl. Cover and chill at least 1 hour or upto 1 day for flavours to mellow.

PANEER DIP

Make a splash at your next party with this creamy, paneer dip.

Ingredients (Makes 2 cups)
- 2 Cups pulpy paneer.
- 2 tbsp mayonnaise.
- 2 tbsp cream.
- 1 tsp Worcestershire sauce, salt and pepper to taste.

Preparation
Beat all the ingredients together until smooth and chill until ready to serve.

Cucumber Dip

This healthy dip has a robust flavour that your guests will rave about.

Ingredients (Makes 3/4 cup)
- 1 large cucumber
- 1/4 cup chopped parsley
- 1 tbsp finely chopped onion
- ¼ cup paneer
- ¼ cup hung curd
- 1 tsp lime juice
- 1 tbsp sugar
- salt and freshly ground pepper to taste
- 1 minced green chilli

Preparation
Peel, deseed and chop the cucumber. Process all the ingredients in a blender until creamy and smooth. Refrigerate for at least 15 minutes before serving.

Hot Schezwan Sauce

If you want to add a professional touch to your parties, serve this hot sauce not only with chinese food, but also kababs and other snacks.

Ingredients

- 100 g whole red chillies
- 50 gm ginger, grated
- 10 cloves of garlic, very finely chopped
- 2 tbsp refined oil
- 1 tbsp chopped celery
- 1 tbsp vinegar
- 3 tbsp tomato ketchup
- 1 tsp sugar, salt to taste
- ½ tsp pepper powder, chopped spring onion for garnishing
- ½ tsp ajinomoto

Preparation

Discard the seeds and soak the red chillies in hot water for half an hour. Grind to a paste.

Heat the oil in a pan. Saute ginger, garlic and celery for 2 minutes. Add the chilli paste and stir fry for another minute, add the rest of the ingredients and saute well.

Remove when thick. Serve garnished with spring onion.

GREEN TOMATO PINEAPPLE DIP

Ingredients (Makes 2 bottles)

- 1 kg green tomatoes
- 1 small can of pineapple
- 1 large onion, chopped
- 2 cups sugar
- 6 green chillies
- 1 cup white vinegar
- 2 tbsp lime juice
- 1 tbsp salt
- 5 chopped glace cherries for garnishing

Preparation

Blanch, deseed and roughly chop the tomatoes. Chop the green chillies and soak in the lime juice for at least two hours.

Drain the pineapple slices, reserving the syrup. Puree the pineapple in a blender and keep aside.

Take out the chillies from the lemon juice and keep the juice aside. Grind the onion and chillies with a little vinegar.

In a stainless steel saucepan, heat the vinegar, sugar, salt, tomatoes, pineapple puree, the syrup and ground paste.

When it comes to a boil, reduce the heat to medium and keep stirring till the mixture attains a thick sauce like consistency. Add the lime juice.

Boil for another couple of minutes. Remove. Garnish with chopped glace cherries. Keep refrigerated.

Orange Sauce

Here's an easy to spread sauce for those who want a little tang with their kababs. Makes an excellent marinade for chicken or meat, too.

Ingredients (Makes 2 cups)

- 1 medium onion, minced
- 2 cloves of garlic minced
- 2 tbsp butter
- 2 tbsp water
- ¼ cup brown sugar
- 1 cup tomato ketchup
- 2 tbsp white vinegar
- 1 tbsp mustard paste
- 2 tbsp worcestershire sauce
- 1 tsp orange rind
- ¼ cup orange juice
- 1 orange

Preparation

Peel the orange. Remove the pips and membrane. Divide into segments.

Saute the onion and garlic in the butter until translucent. Add the water and brown sugar and simmer for 1 minute.

Add the ketchup, vinegar, mustard, worcestershire sauce and orange rind, stirring constantly.

Pour in the orange juice and stir until blended. Simmer over very low heat for 15–20 minutes, stirring occasionally.

Remove and add the orange segment. Let cool and use.

SOM TAM
(RAW PAPAYA SALAD)

This unique salad from Thailand has a surprising ingredient in the form of green papaya. The papaya adds a most welcome fresh and delicate flavour and crunchy texture.

Ingredients (Serves 6)
- 1 green papaya
- 2 green chillies, finely chopped
- 3 tbsp coconut cream
- 150 ml thick coconut milk, grated rind and juice of 1 lime
- 2 tsp palm sugar, powdered
- 2 tbsp Thai fish sauce (optional)
- 2 tbsp coriander leaves

Preparation
Wash, peel, deseed and grate the papaya. Do not wash thereafter.

Mix all the ingredients together in a bowl; cover and refrigerate for at least 2 hours before serving.

Perfect Eggless Mayonnaise

For those who do not eat eggs, I find it even better than the common mayonnaise.

Ingredients

- ½ cup refined oil, 6 tbsp milk powder
- 1/3 cup hot water
- ½ tsp salt, ½ tsp mustard powder, dash of pepper
- 3 tbsp lime juice
- ¼ cup cream (optional)
- 1 tbsp powdered sugar

Preparation

Put the oil, milk powder and water into the blender.

Blend at a low speed until well mixed. Add salt, pepper, mustard, lime juice and sugar.

Blend at high speed till the mayonnaise is thick and smooth. Finally fold in the cream, if using.

Use straight away or store in an airtight jar in the refrigerator.

If you find it thin, add more milk powder; if too thick, add a little hot water. If you add the lime juice at the beginning, you'll find the mayonnaise emulsify faster.

MASALA RAITA

Served with Indian kababs or western type of barbecued foods - this extremely versatile raita will do justice to both.

Ingredients

- 1 cup hung curd
- 1/3 cup cream
- 1 tsp lime juice
- 2 tsp chaat masala
- 2 tbsp powdered sugar or to taste
- 1 tsp roasted and powdered cumin
- ½ tsp chilli powder, black salt to taste, very finely chopped coriander leaves for garnishing

Preparation

Whip the curd with 1 tbsp milk, then fold in the cream. Mix all the remaining ingredients. Taste and adjust seasonings, garnish with coriander leaves, chill and serve.

PEANUT KACHUMBER

Ingredients

- 100 gm roasted peanuts, coarsely crushed.
- 4 tbsp grated coconut.
- 2 tbsp chopped tomatoes.
- 1 small onion, finely chopped.
- 4 green chillis, finely chopped, juice of 1 lime.
- 1 tsp sambhar masala.
- 1 tbsp refined oil.
- ½ tsp mustard seeds.
- 1 sprig curry leaves.
- salt to taste.

Preparation

Mix together the peanuts, coconut, tomatoes, onion, green chillies, lime juice, sambhar masala and salt.

Heat the oil. Temper with mustard seeds and curry leaves. When they sizzle, pour over the Kachumber and serve.

Superior Barbecue Sauce

What's sauce for this is sometimes sauce for that. The following can be used 3 ways. Use it to tenderise the meat, or brush it on meat while it cooks to glaze and keep the original juciness in; or, serve as a sauce.

Ingredients (Makes 2 cups)

- 2 tbsp brown sugar
- 2 tbsp molasses
- 1 tbsp paprika (or kashmiri chilli powder)
- 1 tsp salt
- 1 tsp prepared mustard
- 1 tsp capsico sauce
- ½ tsp chilli powder
- 2 tbsp worcestershire sauce
- ¼ cup vinegar
- 1 cup tomato puree
- ½ cup tomato ketchup
- 1 cup water
- ¼ tsp pepper

Preparation

Combine all ingredients in a saucepan. Bring to a boil. Simmer till thick.

Aam Kasundi
(Mango and Mustard Sauce)

This typically Bengali sauce goes extremely well with spicy kababs.

Ingredients
- 1 kg raw mangoes
- salt to taste
- 250 gm mustard seeds
- 1 cup mustard oil

Preparation

Peel, deseed and dice the raw mangoes. Process in a blender till smooth. Grind the mustard seeds to a powder. Add salt, mustard powder and oil to the mango paste.

Pour the paste in a glass jar and keep in the hot sun for a week. Keeps well for a long time.

Apricot Chutney

Whenever you're making a cooked chutney like this, do not cut down on the quantity of sugar or vinegar as they are the preservative.

Ingredients

- 250 gm dried apricots
- 500 ml malt vinegar
- 125 gm sultanas (stoned)
- 125 gm raisins
- 1 tsp salt, grated rind and juice of 1 lime
- 500 gm of cooking apple
- 500 gm brown sugar

Tie in a muslin
- 4 dry red chillies
- 1 small piece of ginger
- 2 cloves garlic
- 10 peppercorns
- 1 tbsp mustard seeds
- 1 tsp nigella

Preparation

Cut the dried apricots in small pieces, discarding the seeds. Soak in water for 4-5 hours alongwith the sultanas, chopped and raisins.

Peel, core and dice apples. Drain and put the apricots, sultanas and raisins into a stainless steel saucepan with a little of the vinegar and all the other ingredients except apples and sugar. Add the muslin cloth containing the spices.

Boil steadily for 30 minutes adding the vinegar; then add the apple and sugar. Stir until the sugar dissolves.

Boil on medium heat, stirring well for another 30 minutes or until thick. Remove the spice bag squeezing well to extract maximum flavour.

Pour into hot, sterilised jars. put on the lid when the chutney cools.

MASALAS

TANDOORI MASALA

If you prepare the following masalas at home, you'll never buy any from outside.

Ingredients

- 50 gm coriander seeds
- 50 gm cuminseeds
- 50 gm black peppercorns
- 20 gm kasuri methi
- 30 green cardamoms
- 15 cloves
- 5 sticks (2.5 cm long) cinnamon
- 1 tsp ajwain
- 1 tsp mace
- 50 gm black salt
- 20 gm ginger powder
- 20 gm chilli powder

Preparation

The spices should be absolutely dry. Dry grind to a powder. Sieve and powder the residue again. Store in a clean, airtight container. Will keep well for at least 6 months.

TANDOORI CHAAT MASALA

Ingredients

- 50 gm cuminseeds
- 50 gm peppercorns
- 50 gm black salt
- 30 gm dry mint leaves
- 2 tbsp kasuri methi
- 30 green cardamoms
- 15 cloves
- 1 tsp ajwain
- 1 tsp asafeetida
- 1 tsp tartaric powder, a large pinch of mace powder
- 125 gm amchur
- 1 ½ tbsp dry ginger powder
- 1 tbsp chilli powder

Preparation

Put all the ingredients in a blender and grind to a fine powder. Sieve and grind the residue again, if needed. Store in a dry airtight container. Keeps well indefinitely.

GARAM MASALA

It is this garam masala that has been used throughout this book. It is very strong, so use cautiously.

Ingredients

- 25 gm/1½ tbsp green cardamoms
- 25 gm/1½ tbsp cloves
- 25 gm/1½ tbsp cinnamon sticks
- 10 gm/2 tsp caraway seeds
- 10 gm/2 tsp mace
- 10 gm/2 tsp white peppercorns
- 1 nutmeg

Preparation

Roast all the ingredients very lightly on a dry frying pan or tawa. Powder in a blender and store in airtight bottle. Will keep for at least 6 months.

Note: Use either set of measurements. Do not mix the two. For some recipes, it is best to measure accurately. What you can do is buy the ingredients from the market in the required quantities and use them.

GLOSSARY

FOODGRAINS

English	Spiked millet	Barely	Jowar	Italian millet	Maize (dry)	Oatmeal	Ragi
Hindi	Bajra	Jau	Juar-janera	Kangri	Makai	Jai	Okra
Tamil	Cambu	Barli arisi	Cholam	Thenai	Muka cholam	–	Ragi
Telugu	Gantelu	Barli biyyam	Jonnalu	Korralu	Mekka jonnalu	–	Chollu
Marathi	Bajri	Juv	Jwari	Rala	Muka	–	Nachni
Bengali	Bajra	Job	Juar	Syamadhan kangni	Sukna paka bhutta	Jai	–
Gujarati	Bajri	Jau	Juar	Ral kang	Makai	–	Ragi bhav
Malayalam	Kamboo	Yavam	Cholam	Thina	Unakku cholam	Oat mavu	Moothari (korra)
Kannada	–	–	Jola	–	Vonugida musikinu	Jolu	Ragi

Contd...

Foodstuff	Rice (raw)	Rice (parboiled)	Rice (white)	Rice (black)	Rice flakes	Rice (puffed)	Samai
Hindi	Arwa chawal	Usna chawal	Safed chaval	Chaval (kala)	Chowla	Murmura	Kutki, Sanwali
Tamil	Pachai arisi	Puzhungal arisi	Vellai puttu arisi	Karuppu puttu arisi	Arisi aval	Arisia pori	Samai
Telugu	Pachi biyyam	Uppudu biyyam	Thella biyyam	Nalla biyyam	Atukulu	Murmuralu	–
Marathi	Tandool	Tandool ukda	–	–	Pohe	Murmure	Sava
Bengali	Atap chowl	Siddha chowl	–	–	Chaler khood	Muri	Kangni
Gujarati	Hatna	Ukadelloo chokha	–	–	Pohva	Mumra	–
Malayalam	Pacchari	Puzhungal ari	Velutha puttari	Karutha puttari	Avil	Pori	–
Kannada	Kotnuda	Kotnuda	–	–	Avalukki	–	Puri
Kashmiri	–	–	–	–	–	–	–

Contd...

English	Semolina	Vermicelli	Wheat flour (whole)	Wheat flour (whole)	Wheat flour (refined)	Wheat (broken)
Hindi	Sooji	Siwain	Gehun	Atta	Maida	Daliya
Tamil	Ravai	Semiya	Godumai	Muzhu godmai ma	Maida mavu	Godhumbi ravai
Telugu	Rawa	Semiya	Godhumalu	Godhum Pindi	Mqaidha pindi	Dinchina gadhumalu
Marathi	–	Shevaya	Gahu	Gahu kuneek	Gahu kuneek	Gavache satva
Bengali	Suji	Sewai	Gomasta	Atta	Maida	Bhanga gom
Gujarati	–	–	Ghau	Ato	–	Fadia ghaun
Malayalam	Rava	Semiya	Muzhu gothambu	Gothambu mavu	Maidu tha gothambu mavu	Gothambu ari
Kannada	–	Shavige	Godhi	Godhi	Hittu madia	Kuttida Godhi
Kashmiri	–	Ku' nu'	–	–	–	–

VEGETABLES

English	Ash gourd	Bitter gourd	Bottle gourd	Brinjal	Broad beans	Cabbage	Capsicum
Hindi	Safed petha	Karela	Ghia	Baingan	Sem	Bandhgobi	Simla mirch
Bengali	Chal kumdo	Karala	Laoo	Begoon	Sheem	Badha kopee	Lonka
Assamese	Lao bishesh	–	Jati lao	Bengena	Urahi	Bondhakobi	Kashmiri jalakai
Oriya	Pani kakkaru	–	Lau	Baigana	Shimba	Patrokobi	Simla lonka
Marathi	Kohala	Karle	Dudhi	Wangi	Chewda	Pan kobi	Bhopli mirchi
Gujarati	Petha	Karela	Dudhi	Ringna	Papdi	Kobi	Simla marchan
Telugu	Boodie gumadi	Kakara	Sorakaya	Vankaya	Pedda chikkudu	Kosu	Pedda mirappa
Kannada	Budu gumbala	Hagalkai	Sorekai	Badanekai	Chapparadavare	Kosu	Donne menasinakai
Tamil	Pooshanikkai	Pavakkai	Suraikai	Kaththarikai	Avaraikai	Muttaikosu	Kuda milakai
Malayalam	Kumbalanga	Kapakka	Cheraikai	Vazhutheninga	Amarakai	Muttakose	Parangi mulagu
Kashmiri	Masha'ly al	Karelu	–	Waangun	–	Bandgobhi	–

Contd...

English	Carrot	Cauliflower	Cluster beans	Colocasia	Coriander leaves	Cucumber	Curry leaves
Hindi	Gajar	Phulgobi	Guar ki phalli	Arvi	Hara Dhania	Khira	Kadi patta
Bengali	Gujar	Foolcopy	Jhar sim	–	Dhonay pata	Sasha	Curry pata
Assamese	Gajor	Phoolkobi	–	Kochu	Dhania paat	–	Narasingha paat
Oriya	Gajar	Phulakobi	–	–	Dhania patra	–	Bhrusanga patta
Marathi	Gajar	Fulkobi	Govari	Alu kanda	Kothimbir	Kakari	Kadhi patta
Gujarati	Gajar	Fool kobi	Govar	Alvi	Kothmir	Kakdi	Mitho limdo
Telugu	Gajjara	Cauliflower	Goruchikkudu kayalu	Chamadumpa	Kothimeera	Dosakaya	Karivepaku
Kannada	Gajjari	Hookosu	Gorikayi	Keshave	Kottambari soppu	Southaikayi	Karibevu
Tamil	Carrot	Koveppu	Kothavarangai	Seppann kizhangu	Koththamali ilaigal	Kakkarikkai	Kariveppilai
Malayalam	Carrot	Koveppu	Kothavarangai	Seppann kizhangu	Koththamali ilaigal	Kakkarikkai	Kariveppilai
Kashmiri	–	Phoolgobhi	–	–	–	Laa'r	–

English	Drumstick	French beans	Garlic	Ginger (fresh)	Green chillies	Jackfruit	Lady's finger
Hindi	Sahjan ki phali	Pharsbeen	Lassan	Adrak	Hari mirch	Kathal	Bhindi
Bengali	Sajane dauta	French beans	Rasoon	Ada (tatka)	Kancha lonka	Echore	Dhanroce
Assamese	Sajina	Faras been	Naharoo	Ada (kesa)	Kesa jalakia	–	Bhendi
Oriya	Sajana chhuin	French beans	Rasuna	Ada (kancha)	Kancha lonka	Kawla phanas	Bhendi
Marathi	Shevgyachya shenga	Farasbi	Lasun	Aale	Hirvya mirchya	Phunas	Bhendi
Gujarati	Saragavani shing	Fansi	Lasan	Adu	Lila marcha	Letha panasa	Bhinda
Telugu	Munagakayalu	French chikkudu	Vellulli	Allam (pachchi)	Pachchi mirapakayalu	Yele halasu	Bendakaaya
Kannada	Nuggekai	Avare	Bellulli	Ashi Shunti	Hasi menasinakai	Pila pinchu	Bendekai
Tamil	Murungaikai	Beans	Ulli Poondu	Inji	Pachchai milagai	Idichakka	Vendaikai
Malayalam	Muringakkaya	Beans	Veluthulli	Inji	Pachamulagu	–	Vendakka
Kashmiri	–	–	Ruhan	–	Myool martsu waungun		Bindu

English	Lettuce	Lemon	Mint leaves	Onion	Parwal	Peas	Plantain flower	Plantain gree.
Hindi	Salad ke patte	Nimbu	Pudina	Pyaz	Parwal	Matar	Kele ka phool	Kacha kela
Bengali	Lettuce	Lebu	Poodina pata	Pyaz	Potol	Motor	Mocha	Kancha kala
Assamese	Laipaat	Nemu	Podina	–	Patol	Motormah	–	–
Oriya	Lettuce	Lembu	Podana patra	–	Potala	Matar	–	–
Marathi	Saladchi paane	Limbu	Pudina	Kanda	–	Matar	Kel phool	Kele
Gujarati	Lettuce	Limbu	Fudino	Dungli	–	Vatana	Kelphool	Kela
Telugu	Lettuce koora	Nimma	Pudhina koora	Nirulli	–	Bathanedu	Aratipuwu	Arati kayi
Kannada	Lettuce soppu	Nimbu	Pudina sopu	Erulli	–	Betani	Balo mothu	Bala kayi
Tamil	Lettuce keerai	Elumicham pazham	Pudhinaa	Ulli	–	Pattani Payaru	Vazhappoo	Vazhakka
Malayalam	Uvarcheera	Cherunaranga	Pudhinaa	Ulli	–	Pattani Payaru	Vazhappoo	Vazhakka
Kashmiri	Salaad	–	–	Gandu	–	Matar	–	–

Contd...

English	Plantain stem	Potato	Radish	Red pumpkin	Ridge gourd	Snake gourd	Sweet potato	Yam elephant
Hindi	Kele ka tana	Aloo	Muli	Sitaphal	Torai	–	Shakarkand	Zaminkand
Bengali	Thor	Aloo	Mulo	Ronga Koomra	Jhinge	Chichinga	Rangalu	Kham aloo
Assamese	–	Alu	–	Ronga lao	–	–	–	Kaath aloo
Oriya	–	Alu	–	Kakharu	–	–	–	Deshi alu
Marathi	Kelecha khunt	Batate	Mula	Lal bhopla	Dodka	Pudwal	Ratale	Suran
Gujarati	Kelanu thed	Batata	Mula	Kolu	Turai	Pandola	Sakkaria	Suran
Telugu	Arati devva	Bangaala dumpa	Mullangi	Erra gummadi	Beerakai	Potalakayi	Dumpalu	Kanda dumpa
Kannada	Dindu	Aalugadde	Mullangi	Kempu kumbala	Heeraikai	Padavalai	Genasu	Suvarnagadde
Tamil	Vazhaithandu	Urulaikizhangu	Mullangi	Parangikai	Pirrkkankai	Podalangai	Sarkarai valli kizhangu	Chenai kizhangu
Malayalam	Vazhappindi	Uralakkizhangu	Mullangi	Chuvappu mathan	Pecchinga	Padavalanga	Chakkara kizhangu	Chena
Kashmiri	–	Oloo	Muj	Parrimal	Turrelu	–	–	–

English	Bengal gram (whole)	Bengal gram (split)	Black gram (split)	Black gram (whole)	Cornflour	Cow gram	Green gram (whole)
Hindi	Chana	Chana dal	Urad dal	Sabat urad	Makai ka atta	Lobia (bada)	Moong
Bengali	Chola	Banglar chhola	Mashkolair dal	Mashkolai dal	Bhoottar maida	Barbati	Mug
Assamese	-	Buttor dail	Matir dail (phola)	Matir dail (gota)	Makka atta	-	-
Oriya	-	Buta (chhota)	Biri (phala)	Biri (gota)	Makka atta	-	-
Marathi	Hurbhura	Chana dal	Udid dal	Udid	Makyache pith	Kuleeth	Mug
Gujarati	Chana	Chana nidaal	Adad ni dal	Adad	Makai no lot	-	Mag
Telugu	Sanagalu	Senaga pappu	Mina pappu	Minu mulu	Mokkajonnalu (pindi)	Ada chandalu	Pesalu
Kannada	Kadale	Kadale bela	Uddina bela	Uddu	Musukinajolada hittu	Thadaguni	Hesaru kalu
Tamil	Muzhu kadalai	Kadalai paruppu	Ulutham paruppu	Ulundhu	Chola Maavu	Karamani	Pachai payaru
Malayalam	Kadala	Kadala parippu	Uzhunnu parippu	Uzhunnu	Cholapodi	Payar	Cherupayaru
Kashmiri	Chanu	-	Maha	-	-	-	Muang

Contd...

English	Green gram (split)	Horse gram	Kesari dal	Kidney beans	Red gram	Red lentils	Soya bean
Hindi	Moong dal	Kulthi	Lang dal	Rajma	Arhar dal	Masoor dal	Bhat
Bengali	Moog	Kulthi kalai	Khesari	Barbati beej	Arhar dal	Lal masoor (bhanga)	Gari kalai
Assamese	Sevjiy Boot	-	-	Markhowa urahi	Rahor dail	Masoor dail (phola)	-
Oriya	Muga (Phala)	Kuleeth	Lakh dal	Baragudi chhuin	Harada dali	Masura dali (phata)	-
Marathi	Moog dal	Kuleeth	Lakh	-	Tur dal	Masur dal	Soya
Gujarati	Magnidal	Kuleeth	-	-	Tuver dal	Masur dal	Soya
Telugu	Pesaru pappu	Ulavalu	Lamka pappu	-	Kandi pappu	Missu pappu	-
Kannada	Hesare bele	Huruli	-	-	Togar bele	Masur bele	-
Tamil	Pasi paruppu	Kollu	Vattuparuppu	-	Thuvaram parappu	Massor parippu	-
Malayalam	Cherupayar parippu	Muthira	-	-	Thuvaram parappu	Masoor Parippu	Soya bean
Kashmiri	-	-	-	-	-	Musur	-

FRUITS AND DRY FRUITS

English	Almond	Coconut	Currants	Dates	Dry Plums
Hindi	Badam	Nariyal	Mungaqqa	Khajur	Alu bukhara
Bengali	Badam	Narcole	Manaca	Khejoor	Sookno kool
Assamese	Badam	Narikol	Kismis	Khejur	Sukan bogori
Oriya	Badaam	Nadia	Kala kismis	Khajura	Barakoli jateeya phala
Marathi	Badam	Naral	Manuka	Khajur	Alubhukar
Gujarati	Badam	Naliyer	Kalli draksh	Khajoor	Suka Plum
Telugu	Badam	Kobbari kaaya	Endu nalla dhraksha	Kharjoora pandu	–
Kannada	Badami	Tenginakai	Dweepa dharakshi-kappu	Kharjoora	–
Tamil	Badam/vadhumai	Thengai	Karumdhraakshai	Perichampazham	Aalpacota ular pazham
Malayalam	Badam	Nalikeram/Thenga	Karuthamurthiri	Eethapazham	–

Contd...

English	Guavas	Lemon	Orange	Raisins	Walnuts
Hindi	Amrud	Nimbu	Santra	Kishmish	Akhrot
Bengali	Payara	Lebu	Kamla lebu	Kishmish	Akhrot
Assamese	Madhurium	Nemu	Sumothira	Sukan angoor	Akhrot
Oriya	Pijuli	Lembu	Kamala	Kismis	Akhrot
Marathi	Peru	Limbu	Santre	Bedane	Akrod
Gujarati	Jamrukh	Limbu	Santara	Lal draksh	Akrot
Telugu	Jaamapandu	Nimma	Kamala Pandu	Kismis pallu	Aakrot
Kannada	Seebe	Nimbe	Kittale	Dweepadrakshi	Acrota
Tamil	Koyyapazham	Elumicham pazham	Kichlipazham	Ular dhraakshai	Akhrot
Malayalam	Perakkai	Cherunaranga	Madhura naranga	Unakkamunthiri	Akrotandi

129

DRY SPICES

English	Aniseed	Asafoetida	Basil leaves	Bay leaf	Caraway seeds	Cardamom (brown)	Cardamom (green)	Cinnamon
Hindi	Saunf	Hing	Tulse ke patte	Tej patta	Shahjeera	Moti elaichi	Choti elaichi	Dalchini
Bengali	Mowri	Hing	Tulsi pata	Tej pata	Sajeera	Lach (tamate)	Elach (sobooj)	Daroochini
Assamese	Guwamori	Hing	Tulosi paat	Tejpaat	Bilati jira	Ilachi (muga)	Ilachi (sevjia)	Dalcheni
Oriya	Panamahuri	Hengu	Tulasi patra	Teja patra	Sahajira	Aleicha	Gjuratie	Dalachini
Marathi	Badishep	Hing	Tulsichi paney	Tamal patra	Shahjeera	Masala welchi	Welchi (hirvi)	Dalchini
Gujarati	Variyali	Hing	Tulsina pan	Tamal patra	Jiru	Elcho	Lila alchi	Tuj
Telugu	Sopaginja	Inguva	Thulasi akulu	-	Seema sopyginjale	Yalakulu	Yala kulu (pachavi)	Dalchina chekka
Kannada	Sopubeeja	Hingu	Tulasi ele	-	Caraway beejagalre	Yalakki	Yalakki (hasunu)	Dalchini
Tamil	Perumjeerakam	Perungaayam	Thulasi	-	Karunjeerakam	Elakkai (Pazhuppu)	Elakkai (pachchai)	Lavangapattai
Malayalam	Perumjeerakam	Kaayam	Tulasi	-	Karunjeerakam	Elakkaya	Pach Elakkaya	Karuvapatta
Kashmiri	-	Yangu	-	-	-	Aal budu'a aal	-	-

Contd...

English	Cloves	Coriander seeds	Cumin seeds	Fenugreek seeds	Mace	Mustard seeds	Nutmeg	Parsley
Hindi	Laung	Sukha dhania	Jeera	Methi dana	Javitri	Rai	Jaiphal	Ajmooda ka patta
Bengali	Labango	Dhonay	Jeera	Methi	Jaeetri	Sarsay	Jaifall	Parsley
Assamese	Long	Dhania guti	Gota jeera	Paleng	Janee	Sarioh guti	Jaaiphal	Sugandhi lota
Oriya	Labanga	Dhania	Jira	Methi	jayatree	Sorisha	Jaiphala	Balabalua shaga
Marathi	Lavanga	Dhane	Jire	Methi dane	Jaypatri	Mohari	Jayphal	Ajmoda
Gujarati	Laving	Dhana	Jeeru	Methi	Jaypatra	Rai	Jaypal	Ajmo
Telugu	Lavangalu	Dhaniyalu	Jeelakara	Menthulu	Japathri	Aavaalu	Jaikaaya	Kothimeerajati koora
Kannada	Lavanga	Kottambari beeja	Jeerige	Menthe	Japatri	Sasive kalu	Jaika	Kottambari jotiya soppu
Tamil	Kraambu	Koththamalli virai	Jeerakam	Vendhayam	Jaadipathri	Kadugu	Jaadhikai	Kothamalu ilaigal pole
Malayalam	Karayaamboovu	Kothamalli	Jeerakam	Uluva	Jathipathri	Kadugu	Jathikka	Malliela pole
Kashmiri	Ru'ang	Daaniwal	Zyur	-	Jalwatur	-	Zaaphal	-

Contd...

English	Peppercorns	Pomegranate seeds	Poppy seeds	Red Chillies	Tamarind	Turmeric	Vinegar	Thymol
Hindi	Kali mirch ke daane	Anardana	Khus khus	Lal mirch	Imli	Haldi	Sirka	Ajwain
Bengali	Marich	Dareem bij	Posto	Paka lonka	Tentool	Halood	Seerka	–
Assamese	Jaluk	Dalim guti	–	Sukan jalakia	Teteli	Halodhi	Sirika	–
Oriya	Golamaricha	Dalimba manji	–	Nali lankamaricha	Tentuli	Haladi	Vinegar	–
Marathi	Kale Miri	Dalimbache dane	Khas khas	Lal mirchya	Chincha	Halad	Sirka	Onva
Gujarati	Mari	Dadamna bee	Khaskhas	Lal marcha	Amli	Haldar	Sirko	Ajmo
Telugu	Miriyaalu	Daanimma ginjalu	Gasagasaalu	Erra mirapa kayalu	Chinthapandu	Pasupu	–	–
Kannada	Menasina kalu	Dalimbo beeja	Gasagase beeja	Kempu menasinakai	Hunase hannu	Arasina	–	–
Tamil	Milagu	Maadhulai vidhai	Kasakasaa	Milagai vatal	Puli	Manjal	Pulikaadi	–
Malayalam	Kurumulagu	Madhala naranga kuru	Kaskas	Chuvanna Mulagu	Puli	Manjal	Vinagiri	–

131

Books on
Cookery

60/-

101 Ways to Prepare Curries
—*Aroona Reejhsinghani*
Demy Size • Pages: 136

60/-

101 Chinese Recipes
—*Aroona Reejhsinghani*
Demy Size • Pages: 112

80/-

101 Ways to Prepare Soups & Salads
—*Aroona Reejhsinghani*
Demy Size • Pages: 86

80/-

60/-

101 All Time Savoury Snacks
—*Elizabeth Jyothi Mathew*
Price: Rs. 60/-
Demy Size • Pages: 104

101 Mix & Match Recipes with Vegetables
—*Satarupa Banerjee*
Demy Size • Pages: 143

Books on
Cookery

Rice Bonanza
— *Manjira Majumdar*
Small Size • Pages: 144 (colour)

125/-

80/-

**Paneer
Bonanza**
— *Prabhjot Mundhir*
Small Size • Pages: 168

Rice Bonanza
— *Sangeeta Gupta*
Small Size • Pages: 152 (colour)

125/-

96/-

**Nutritious
Mushroom Recipes**
— *Prabhjot Mundhir*
Small Size • Pages: 128 (colour)

Postage:
Rs. 15/- on
each book
Every subsequent
book Rs. 5/- extra

Books on
Cookery

80/-

60/-

Cooking Made Easy
— *Deepa S. Phatak, Shyam Phatak*
Demy Size • Pages: 104

Modern Cookery Book
— *Asha Rani Vohra*
Demy Size • Pages: 144

80/-

80/-

Over 100
Fat-Free Recipes
— *Elizabeth Jyothi Mathew*
Demy Size • Pages: 120

Dishes and Deserts
— *Tanushree Podder*
Demy Size • Pages: 104

Postage:
Rs. 15/- on
each book

Every subsequent
book Rs. 5/- extra

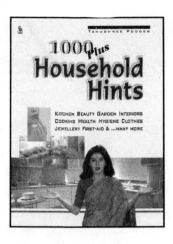

1000 Plus Household Hints
—Tanushree Podder

With the disintegration of the traditional joint family system, women have found it difficult to carry on with household chores without the guidance of the elder women of the household. As a result, women are forced to learn through the trial and error, which is not only time consuming, but also incurs a lot of wastage.

Many books are written on different subjects but not many books have been written on handling the common problems faced by a young home-maker when she first sets up her home.

This book is the result of careful compilation of ideas and tips by the author in neat sections. The common problems faced by a young home-maker when she first sets up her home are enlisted and remedies provided to eliminate them.

The book becomes relevant in the present era because most young women are working and have neither the time nor the opportunity to go around hunting for hints.

The book provides tips on: ❖ Cooking ❖ Cleaning ❖ Skin Care ❖ Storing ❖ Gardening ❖ Jewellery Care

Big Size • Pages: 180
Price: Rs. 120/- • Postage: Rs. 20/-

Smart Housekeeping
for the woman of today
—Rupa Chatterjee

A housewife is very often judged by the way she keeps her house. For her it's like a temple—a key through which she can ensure highest level of physical and emotional comfort for her family.

And in view of its critical significance in one's life, it's imperative that your home is managed well—an art every homemaker needs to master.

This book, written by a seasoned housewife, who is also a professional interior designer, is one such handy help that deals with the subject in a critical and comprehensive manner. Never before have so many tips and suggestions, covering every aspect of the subject, been put together in a single volume. From interior decoration, time management, organising household chores, cleaning of house and its security, maintaining of gadgets and household articles to household budget, etiquette for all occasions, first aid, travel and transfer, personal grooming, it goes on to cover tips on energy conservation and interpersonal relationship.

A must for all who wish to make their home a paradise.

Big Size • Pages: 296
Price: Rs. 150/- • Postage: 20/-

Smart Housekeeping
for the Woman of Today

1000 Plus
Household Hints